LAVISH ABSENCE

Lavish Absence:
Recalling and Rereading Edmond Jabès

Rosmarie Waldrop

Wesleyan University Press

MIDDLETOWN, CT

Published by Wesleyan University Press, Middletown, CT 06459

Printed in the United States of America 5 4 3 2 1

Library of Congress Cataloging-in-Publication Data
Waldrop, Rosmarie.
Lavish absence : recalling and rereading Edmond Jabès / Rosmarie Waldrop.
p. cm.
Includes bibliographical references.
ISBN 0–8195–6579–2 (alk. paper)—ISBN 0–8195–6580–6 (pbk. : alk. paper)
1. Jabaes, Edmond—Criticism and interpretation. I. Title.
PQ2619.A112 Z95 2002
841'.914—dc21 2002014911

A section of this book has been printed in *JUDAISM: A Quarterly Journal of Jewish Life & Thought.*

The author would like to thank The Lila Wallace-Reader's Digest Fund for a Writer's Award.

Book design by Dean Bornstein

CONTENTS

FOREWORD

"Our decision to write, to talk, springs from a lack," Edmond Jabès observes in one of his discussions with Marcel Cohen (DB 54).* Loss is the writer's constant companion, present as his imagination nomadically crosses the sands of the desert he has left behind, as his words wander through the books that silence them, as his cries are swallowed up by the unrelenting endlessness of suffering, as his speech weakens before the immensity of the unspeakable, as his thoughts are blanched to nothingness by the margins they bleed into, as his writing collides with the impossibility of knowledge and his being with the impermanence of life and the horror of history.

Loss is the translator's constant companion as well. It is present as her mind struggles to find "foreign" words for a discourse of questions, quotations, aphorisms, and fragments, already from their conception in exile from the native soil of their birth, as her consciousness takes up residence in that in-between space—a terrain of strangeness, exile, and indeterminacy—separating two languages, and as her knowledge of words and syntax fights to preserve meanings that the fundamental difference between languages irreversibly effaces once and for all. What is lost in translation is lost twice over, because the original text has already internalized the loss it has had to confront in order to speak, the silence it has had to absorb in order to come into being, the absence it has had to face in order to make itself present, and the death it has had to pass through in order to live. Writing and translation are, as Edmond Jabès and Rosmarie Waldrop know first-hand, a "*lavish* absence"—the "richness of utter poverty" (PLS 81), as Jabès writes—in which the sumptuousness of a language tries desperately to fill a void, in which the excess of a speech confronts endless silence and its own "darkened splinter-echo" (Paul Celan, "Das Gedunkelte," *Schneepart*), in which the torrent of letters, words, spaces, pages, chapters, and

* See pages 157–158 for a list of abbreviations of the works of Edmond Jabès and their translations.

books flows profusely in a vain effort to write the inexpressible absent Book of absence. In the unending act of translation—for there will always be *other* words, *other* sentences, *other* syntactical forms, *other* roads not taken—is reflected the unending act of writing. The book, as Edmond Jabès, once wrote, "closes always on a lost face" (PLS 58): that of the word not found, that of the meaning on the other side of language, that of the book yet to be written, that of the loved one gone forever in whose place resides a deep, even a lavish, grief.

Rosmarie Waldrop's *Lavish Absence* begins and ends with a lost face: the wise furrowed brow, the sparkling, impish, blue eyes, the dark eyebrows, the high cheekbones, the carefully combed hair, the full mouth breaking quickly into an indulgent smile of extreme gentleness and sweetness, the handsome Valentino profile of Edmond Jabès. But loss has been her métier since she began in an act of friendship a translation that would soon reveal itself an act of *love*. No other word can account for her faithfulness to Edmond Jabès's writing, for her commitment to the complex, difficult forms of his discourse—the abundance of meditations, stories, poems, prayers, echoes, graffiti, dialogues, invocations, commandments, fables, songs, threnodies, hymns, cries, silences—for her dogged pursuit of his "lean word, haggard, wandering, insulted, burned, beleaguered, bleeding" (BYRP 218), and for her courage in transporting an entire oeuvre, with the inevitable sea changes such a voyage demands, into English. Fearlessly, she has wandered with Edmond Jabès across the endless reaches of his prose, the desert sands of his writing, looking ahead to the footprints he has left, but almost as quickly losing them in the blinding light and the shifting dunes of the landscape of writing, and out of necessity turning to look back at the new footprints she, alone, has laid down during her journey. These after-prints of her passage are the traces out of which her translations emerge.

Lavish Absence offers more than a subtle and learned reading of Edmond Jabès's work, more than an honest and candid study of the difficulty of translation, more than a philosophical meditation on language and writing, and more than a personal history of a dialogue of many years' duration between two friends and between two languages. It brings back to life the "lost face" of Edmond Jabès: his laugh, his jokes, his gestures, his body language, his sartorial elegance, his warm and generous friendships with others, his hatred of racism, his lightness and gravity, his great love for Arlette, his extraordinary wife, and for his daughters Viviane and Nimet, his exile from Egypt, his difficult years starting a new life in Paris, his journeys to the United States, Italy, and other countries, his anxiety over travel, his apartment on the rue de l'Epée-de-Bois, the paintings he loved, the books he read, and the objects he collected.

Yet, sadly, the face of Edmond Jabès must of necessity be lost in translation, for all that can ultimately remain of it are words: memories and images translated into language. We who grieve his absence do so perhaps lavishly, through writing, there being no other way. His words and our words—those that come to us as we read his words or think about his life—produce a dialogue; but it is a dialogue that wanders endlessly, that circles its subject never reaching the center of his being. Death bequeaths language to us, telling us to fill with more and more words the hole that loss has opened in the fabric of our lives. It initiates an absence in the shadow of which no presence can dwell other than the concrete *thereness* of words in all their imprecision and instability as traces of what once existed. The experience of death, loss, and absence, which Edmond Jabès's passing has given us, is the same one that he had already represented in his books. "The word," he writes, "can only live within death" (ELLB 72); "the highest ambition of writing would then be the desperate attempt to experience its death" (YEA 209); the book is the "place where language faces the void wherein it ceases to have meaning, pointing no longer to anything but Nothingness" (PLS 40). Experiencing the presence of death in and through his writing, Edmond Jabès had already with majestic courage lived his death. The endless pursuit of one book toward another, the depleting and silencing of one text so that the next one could take its place, the marching forward into the void of fragment after fragment in book after book indicate Edmond Jabès's unblinking acceptance of the death that grounds all of life.

"All writers want the word to be flesh," Rosmarie Waldrop remarks. "The flesh of a bird, so it can take wing. Now the flesh has become words. And the words live among us." But words—oh, if they could only be!—are not flesh. Edmond Jabès's books are not Edmond Jabès. And yet, sadly indeed, they *are*. For Edmond Jabès now coincides only with the body of words he has written. The Book of Edmond Jabès is closed forever, even though we can continually open *The Book of Questions, The Book of Resemblances, The Book of Dialogue, The Book of Shares, The Book of Margins, The Book of Hospitality*. Therein lies the tragic paradox of writing, as Edmond Jabès recognized. Writing replaces life, fossilizes being, arrests time, *unless*, it remains focused on and makes a space within itself for death: the death that undoes certainty and truth, the death that privileges the unanswerable question, the death that erodes the book so that on the site of its destruction a new, ephemeral, mortal, and uncertain text can rise. The Book must never be closed if life is to remain open. For the man Edmond Jabès this is no longer possible. But for us, the readers of Edmond Jabès, the book will stay open; it will look forward to the unread book; it will force us to wander endlessly in the unstable terrain of language and make us accept the indeterminacy of truth, the precariousness of knowledge, and the fragility of existence, as Edmond Jabès, the writer, did when he was Edmond Jabès, the man.

The presence of Edmond Jabès, this loving, generous man, haunts his writing in absentia, lavishly in absentia. It also haunts, as a series of images, stories, anecdotes, and words, the memories of those who met him. Three months before his death on January 2, 1991, Edmond and Arlette Jabès visited the old synagogue (now an historical monument) in the Andalusian city of Cordoba, where Edmond had gone to give a reading of his work. During their visit, the guardian of the synagogue, the third of three generations of non-Jews to watch over the synagogue, rushed up to Edmond, whose reading he had attended, and passionately told the writer: "For centuries this synagogue has had no voice. Now, it echoes with yours." Taking a photograph of Edmond and Arlette, he promised them that he would place it on the wall above his bed "so that it will always be close to me."

Edmond Jabès still remains close but as an image, a memory, a word weakly trying to translate the silence into which he has fallen.

Or perhaps this silence reverberates with a question, a question once asked by Socrates and inscribed in stone on the inside walls of the temple in the cemetery of Père Lachaise, where Edmond Jabès's cremation ceremony took place a few days after his death: "The hour has come for us to part. I to die, you to live. Who of us has the better lot?" It was perhaps fitting that Edmond Jabès's remains be laid to rest on the wings of a question to which no human answer can ever be given.

This man of the book who wrote so many different books, all moving endlessly toward an impossible Book, distant, silent, indefinable, unwritable, died while reading a book. A few months after his good friend Michel Leiris had passed away in 1990, Edmond had an intriguing dream. Walking in the Jardin du Luxembourg one splendid day he meets Leiris who says to him, "Edmond, I didn't expect to see you so quickly." Several months later, sitting in an armchair in his living room at the beginning of the new year, Edmond picks up from a pile of books lying beside him a posthumous work by Leiris *(Fissures)*, which the publisher had just sent him. It is this book that has already fallen to the floor when Arlette, returning from the kitchen several minutes later, finds Edmond slumped in his chair.

"There are," Edmond Jabès once wrote, "no words for adieu" (ET 79). But it is this very lack that gives birth to an endless sequence of words, the way grief provokes an unstoppable flow of tears. It is as if language were looking for that impossible mot juste that might finally say "adieu." Writing is lavish only because absence is so profound and ultimately unspeakable.

RICHARD STAMELMAN
Norwich, Vermont

LAVISH ABSENCE

☘ ☘ ☘

No matter where, in cafés, in the métro, while walking, at dinner, on little bits of paper, on matchbooks, napkins, on his memory, Edmond Jabès writes. Because life is a book that needs to be written at any moment.

All his life he practices death, the death at the end of each book, each poem, when the work no longer needs the author and rejects him. Now absorbed into his books. With all his body.

"The writer is nobody," he says.

As if he would prepare us for his absence.

Edmond Jabès walks, slowly, hands crossed in back, with the steady steps of the nomad, steps sown by the desire of words to come together, the rhythm of question and further question, the cadence of commentary.

•

> Man does not exist. God does not exist. The world alone exists through God and man in the open book.

Energy, matter. It exists, but it becomes "world" only in the book, in language, which is created by man and at the same time creates him. "You are the one who writes and is written" stands at the beginning of *The Book of Questions*. Faced with an undecipherable world we set out to create language, a place where human discourse can arise, and we come to exist as human beings; where, at the same time, we can maintain a relation to what transcends us, the undecipherable, the ultimate otherness, and speak to it under the name of God.

Matter becomes the matter of words, which creates structure, makes legible, interprets, against a ground of unreadable silence.

> We know of silence only what words can tell us. Whether you like it or not, we ratify only the word.

•

There are key words, says Edmond Jabès, that engender the book. Obsessive words, words we cannot get rid of. Words that cannot be emptied of meaning: *God, Jew, Law, Eye, Name, Book*. And graves. His mother's in Bagneux, his father's in Milan, his brother's in Rome.

> Four graves. Three countries. Does death know borders? One family. Two continents. Four cities. Three flags. One language: of nothingness. One pain.

A book about "God and the world." About everything. A book sui generis: an untold story forms the pre-text for rabbinical commentaries, poems, aphorisms, word-play with philosophical implications, and reflective, densely metaphorical prose. Shifting voices and constant breaks of mode let silence have its share and allow for a fuller meditative field than possible in linear narrative or analysis.

A book about the word. Between scream and silence. The word through which we become human. Other. The word which is our mirror and our wound.

•

> Mark the first page of the book with a red marker for in the beginning the wound is invisible.

These words open *The Book of Questions*. In the beginning is the wound. Invisible. Are we on familiar Freudian territory? Is it the artist's wound, the irritation that causes the pearl, the original lesion that the artist's work forever tries to repair?

More than the artist's wound, it is the wound of the Jew. Sarah deported to a concentration camp, Sarah gone mad, Sarah incarnating Israel's scream of suffering. And Yukel unable to go on living.

The wound of circumcision is metaphysical and existential. It is a wound we all share. The Jew has been persecuted for being "other." But "otherness" is the condition of individuation, the condition of being set apart from the rest of creation in the glorious—and murderous—species of humankind and, in addition, set apart from our fellow humans as individuals, always "other."

Judaism: a paradoxically collective experience of individuation. Exemplary of the human condition.

Let us not forget, says Jabès, that "if we say 'I' we already say *difference*."

•

A metaphorical Judaism:

> And Serge Segal shouted at the prisoners around him, who would soon be scattered in the various extermination camps prepared for them, shouted as if in the name of the Lord to His assembled people: "You are all Jews, even the anti-Semites, because you are all marked for martyrdom."

But who is not a victim? Death awaits us all, even the hangman. And sure enough: "Ah, the dead are all Jewish" because "[w]ho could be more of a stranger than a dead man?"

Doubly Jewish then, in his death. But already in his lifetime, Edmond Jabès had carried otherness one step farther, into the double isolation of the *unbelieving* Jew:

> "Rejected by your people, robbed of your heritage: who are you?" . . .
>
> "If you make no difference between a Jew and a non-Jew, are you, in fact, still a Jew?" . . .
>
> I beat my breast with my fist and thought:
>
> "I am nothing.

"My head is cut off.
"But is one man not as good as another?
"The beheaded as good as the believer?"

"The writer is nobody." And the unbelieving Jew?

How could we find ourselves different and not ask questions, not reflect, not speak? All of Edmond Jabès's books are about the word. It is through the word we both question and define ourselves. We live in a semiotic universe. Our lives are books: "You are the one who writes and the one who is written." Writers join the Jews; both are people of the book:

> I talked to you about the difficulty of being Jewish, which is the same as the difficulty of writing. For Judaism and writing are but the same waiting, the same hope, the same wearing down.

One and the same wearing down. "Defeat is the price agreed on."

•

In 1971, Keith Waldrop and I spend a year in Paris, on fellowships. In January, George Tysh, poet, editor of *Blue Pig,* and a former student of Keith's, finds us. He has been working in a Paris gallery for some time and often arranges readings for American poets who pass through. One of our two rooms is fairly large, so for a while the readings take place there.

To one of them—David Rosenberg and the French Canadian Robert Hébert are reading—Claude Royet-Journoud and Anne-Marie Albiach come. Claude notices *Le Livre des Questions* in our bookcase:

"Have you just bought this?"

"No," Keith explains, "we brought it along because Rosmarie has started translating it."

At this Claude rushes across the room to me:

"I must kiss you because you are translating Jabès," and immediately tries to call Jabès on the phone.

I had translated about fifty pages and sent them, with a description of the book, to twenty American publishers. All declined on the grounds that translations had always lost them money.

If the writer is nobody the translator is nobody twice over and, if also lacking a publisher, approaches the cube of nothingness. I had not tried to meet Edmond Jabès. I was discouraged. I was not sure I would continue. But I had brought the book along in case I got stuck in my own work.

The next afternoon, Claude brings Edmond Jabès. A slight body. A deeply lined face, extraordinary blue eyes. Eyes that seem to be moving outward, toward me. Searching. A sense of gentleness, decorum, and warmth.

I give him what I have translated.

A few days later he says he recognizes himself in the rhythm.

Later I tease him: I might not have gone on translating if Claude had not kissed me.

•

I had half expected a severe ascetic. I come to know a man with an enormous sense of humor, a man who loves food, tells jokes, who at the drop of a hat improvises parodies and skits, who plays the clown for his grandchildren. *Faire l'idiot*, he calls it. A man who cultivates lightness because he knows gravity?

But I am not really surprised. There are little chuckles on many a page:

"The Jew answers every question with another question." One of the disciples is driven to despair when he learns that every question only leads to more questions. When he asks: then why should we begin? the Rabbi turns the joke back on him: "You see," said Reb Mendel, "at the end of an argument, there is always a decisive question unsettled."

•

Now I repeat to myself:

Privé d'R, la mort meurt d'asphyxie dans le mot.

Deprived of the air of its *r*, *la mort,* death, dies asphyxiated in the word, *le mot.*

•

. . . the aphorism . . . comes from a need to surround the words with whiteness in order to let them breathe. As you know I suffer from asthma, and sometimes breathing is very difficult for me. By giving breath to my words, I often have the feeling that I am helping myself breathe. *(Interview with Paul Auster)*

•

I follow Edmond Jabès through the streets of Paris, through the sentences of *The Book of Questions*. Some I know by heart. I prepare to usurp his name. In another language.

My—the translator's—relation to the author seems to double—ape, compound—the author's relation to his character in *The Book of Questions:*

> Who are you, Yukel?
> Who will you be?
> "You" means, sometimes, "I."
> I say "I," and I am not "I." "I" means you, and you are going to die. You are drained.
> From now on, I will be alone. . . .
> And it is I who force you to walk. I sow your steps.
> And I think, I speak for you. I choose and cadence.
> For I am writing
> and you are the wound.
> Have I betrayed you, Yukel?
> I have certainly betrayed you.

In dreams, we are everything: the dreamer and all that is dreamed—persons, things, surroundings, events, says Kleist. But I translate while fully awake, fully conscious of the two incompatibilities I try to wrestle together. Of the resistance on both sides.

•

Haroldo de Campos has written a flamboyant essay on translation: "If translation has no muse [as Walter Benjamin had observed], one could however say that it has an angel." This angel is Lucifer, and a good translation should by rights be called a "transluciferation." Why? Not just because Lucifer is the Angel of Light, but because the translator, like Lucifer, says *non serviam*. He says *no* to the "seemingly natural relationship postulated between form and content" in which the content is considered dominant in the way of an "inner presence" or spirit.

Benjamin's "Task of the Translator" had already scoffed at this emphasis as "an inaccurate transmission of an inessential content." For "what does a literary work 'say'? Its essential quality is not statement or the imparting of information."

So what do I want to serve? Clearly the whole. The form in the large sense—not a rhyme scheme or anything else that could be detached from the work, but the way in which the work is inscribed into its language and tradition, its intentionality, Benjamin's "Art des Meinens." Form in the sense of what could not have been written in English. So that translating is an act of exploration. A double exploration, for the translator must not only explore the original, but also search the target language for an idiom, a language within language, that can accommodate the original's "Art des Meinens." For Emmanuel Hocquard, the translator/explorer finds a "blank spot on the map of [in his case] French . . . a particular language within French, which resembles French without being altogether French." So that the exploration actually means "gaining ground," gaining new territory between languages.

•

Edmond Jabès walks slowly. "He is counting the steps between himself and his life." No one is at one with him- or herself. We are "the kernel of a severance," *le noyau d'une rupture*. Reflection internalizes the separation. The mirror in the brain launches us on a search of the self as difficult, as impossible, as the search of the other.

Reflection. Broken light. A self-conscious activity. Jabès cannot tell a simple story any more than he can imagine a simple God. Like Musil, like most contemporary writers, he has lost confidence in the narrative thread, in the continuity of temporal and causal sequence. It is the very substance of the story that crumbles into a pretext for aphorisms, poems, dialogues. A pre-text that is not actually written. A meta-story emerging from the commentaries on it, out of shifting voices, out of breaks within one voice.

•

The breaks are tangible, not only in the shifts from prose to verse or from one voice to another. They are there in the layout of the page. Gaps. Blank spaces that are perhaps what hold the books together, what replace the narrative thread. They let the book show through, the white of the page, of space.

It is more than a matter of typography and layout. Space and the visual have invaded the very basis of the time-based art of language. Of course they have, we say, ever since texts have been written down. But here we are made aware of it. And of the consequences. It is space that makes possible the mirror stage, the gap between seeing and the seen, between object and representation, me and my image, me and others. These blank spaces in Jabès remind us of our condition of separation, of solitude.

Whereas sound envelops. We lose ourselves in music, in recitation. Even in a novel. The "thread of narration" can lead us into an illusion of being part of a seamless world. Or, as Edmond Jabès says, "Through the ear, we shall enter the invisibility of things."

> To abandon oneself to a rhythm is momentarily to cease positing the existence of the surrounding world. . . . Rhythmizing consciousness thus emerges as a *fascinated* consciousness, subject to a fatal, horizonless future. (Nicolas Abraham, *Rhythms*)

It is in the gap, in separation, in the silence that challenges our existence, that we are human.

It is in music that we dream of an original unity.

It is in the tension between these two that Jabès's writing lives. The use of space in the service of consciousness and the magic, the music of sound. This tension establishes its own rhythm, which avoids the pitfall of "fascination."

Josh Cohen, following Joseph Kronick, sees a different function for Jabès's white space: "If writing is to remain faithful to the divine interdiction of representation, it must put itself under perpetual erasure. It is in terms of this function that we must understand the insistent interspersion of white space throughout Jabès's books; whiteness is the mark of an erasure . . ."

So when the artist Robert Groborne marks out, or at least makes illegible, the lines of *Le Livre des Ressemblances* by overwriting, he seems not to understand that the book already contains its own erasure. I would, however, argue that a "representation" in writing can hardly fall under the interdiction because language already negates the material presence of what it names and is thus on the side of death, nothingness, abstraction rather than on the side of idolatry.

•

> As for this distribution of long and short passages, it's a question of rhythm. This is very important to me. A full phrase, a lyrical phrase, is something that has great breath, that allows you to breathe very deeply. There are other times when the work folds in on itself, and the breath becomes shorter, breathing becomes difficult. They say that Nietzsche wrote aphorisms because he suffered from atrocious headaches that made it impossible for him to write very much at any one sitting. Whether this is true or not, I do believe that a writer works with his body, and the book is above all the book of your body. . . . As you know I suffer from asthma . . ."
>
> *(Interview with Paul Auster)*

•

Against Adorno's "after Auschwitz, one can no longer write poetry," Edmond Jabès declares—and practices: "Yes, one can. And, furthermore, one has to." But as he explains to Marcel Cohen, in

From the Desert to the Book, we cannot write in the same manner as before: "One has to write out of that break, out of that unceasingly revived wound."

•

As we cross the Seine, Edmond Jabès begins to speak of Paul Celan. Who threw himself into the Seine. A year ago, in 1970. The pain is still fresh for Edmond, who feels close to Celan even though he cannot read German. He remembers Celan's voice reading to him while he followed along with a translation. He could not relate the two. But he sensed Celan's love-hate for the German he wrote in.

He recalls the day when Celan came to see him with a copy of *The Book of Questions*, heavily annotated in the margins. They talked about the book. Suddenly Celan said:

"No, I will not translate you."

Edmond is a bit taken aback: "But—"

Celan interrupts, vehemently: "No, I cannot."

". . . but I didn't ask you to. I am already happy you read the book."

They go on talking, but every once in a while Celan interjects:

"I will *not* translate you."

Jabès feels he shares Celan's wound. The wound of the artist, the wound of the Jew. But as I read Chris Chen: "the quality of silence in these [Celan's] poems no longer refers only to absent divinity but to absent humanity," I feel he pinpoints a difference between Celan and Jabès. In spite of the horrors of our century, Jabès does not totally despair of human beings.

Jabès and Celan spent an afternoon together shortly before Celan's suicide. Edmond sensed that Celan was disturbed, but perhaps because he was preoccupied himself, no real conversation, no real dialogue, came about.

> That day. The last. Paul Celan at my house. Sitting in this chair that I have right now been staring at for a long time.

Exchange of words, closeness. His voice? Soft, most of the time. And yet it is not his voice I hear today, but his silence. It is not him I see, but emptiness, perhaps because, on that day, each of us had unawares and cruelly revolved around himself.

•

I ask Edmond Jabès:

"You say you are an atheist. How can you constantly write of God?"

"It's a word my culture has given me."

Then he expands:

"It is a metaphor for nothingness, the infinite, for silence, death, for all that calls us into question. It is the ultimate otherness." Or, as he puts it later, in the conversations with Marcel Cohen: "For me the words 'Jew' and 'God' are, it is true, metaphors. 'God' is the metaphor for emptiness; 'Jew' stands for the torment of God, of emptiness."

This God, this unbeliever's God, I can work with.

The very condition of His freedom: *not to be.*

This phrase from *The Book of Margins* is also a perfect definition of potentiality (Aristotle's *dunamis*) which must always include the potential not to *(adunamia)*. I do not recall Edmond Jabès using the term *puissance* itself, but it is for me the most helpful concept in understanding his infinite, his God, his "original Book," especially if we remember that potentiality can never be totally actualized, so that it is a paradoxical presence of what remains absent.

Elsewhere:

To write as if addressing God. But what to expect from nothingness where any word is disarmed?

". . . Truth is the void," replied Reb Mendel.

"If the truth which is in man is void," continued the oldest disciple, "we are nothing in a body of flesh and skin. Therefore God, who is our truth, is also nothing?"

"God is a question," replied Reb Mendel. "A question which leads us to Him who is Light through and for us, who are nothing."

If "God" is a word his culture has given him, it is also a word his *language* has given him: *Dieu*. Jabès's writing unlocks unsuspected riches within this word, unfolds its sounds and letters into a multitude of other words (without regard to etymology and only secondarily to meaning). In *Dieu* he finds the void (*vide*) as well as life (*vie*), of eyes (*d'yeux*). His place (*lieu*) rhymes with His name and is the heavens (*cieux*), that is to say nowhere except in rhyme—and in silence, since "D turns C at the first touch of the eraser." *Dieu* imposes mourning (*deuil*) whose eye (*oeil*) is death.

Dieu = Vide = Vie d'yeux.

God = Emptiness = Life of the eyes.

He said: "God is empty of emptiness. God is the life of emptiness. He is empty of any life of the eyes. Death cries her eyes out, mourning."

Cieux, "the heavens," a plural composed of *ciel* and *yeux*, "heaven" and "eyes."

Dieu is also in the word *Cieux,* as a unique silence: in the mirror of the page, *D* turns *C* at the first touch of the eraser.

Thus "heavens" is the silent plural of "God."

Dieu. Di eu. Dis (à) eux. The empty space between two syllables turns God into "tell them." God lets us tell our grief, our mourning [*deuil*].

You use "God" and "Gods," "Place" and "Places" interchangeably. Because God is many Gods within God, many Places within the Place.

All mourning [*deuil*] mourns, above all, God.

Elsewhere, dice (*dé*) and desire (*désire*) are also revealed to be part of *Dieu*.

> "Do you know that the final period of the book is an eye," he said, "and without lid?"
>
> *Dieu*, "God," he spelled *D'yeux*, "of eyes." "The 'D' stands for desire," he added. "Desire to see. Desire to be seen."
>
> God resembles His Name to the letter, and His Name is the Law.

•

"The name of God is the juxtaposition of all the words in the language," Edmond Jabès reminds Marcel Cohen. "Each word is but a detached fragment of that name."

This Kabbalistic idea means that breaking open words and recombining their letters is neither just fun nor impious. It is not even just the Kabbalistic tradition of "traveling inside the word." For Edmond Jabès, this method "permits a rediscovery, a rereading of the word. One opens a word as one opens a book: it is the same gesture." More, it is creation in the sense of enacting the possible. The motor of this process becomes, as Joseph Guglielmi has realized, the single letter. It at the same time interprets and creates:

> The imperious mobilisation of the letter in the course of its conflict with the word . . . becomes the cardinal moment of Jabès's project. In other terms, the letter is promoted to being the motor of the production of meaning and at the same time the propagator of what is unknown and exempt of meaning.

In *From the Desert to the Book*, Edmond Jabès comments that the absence of vowel points in the traditional Hebrew texts requires special attention from the reader, who must himself become creator (in the absence of God, who is the point from which everything begins?) and create the words:

> In Hebrew, the point is the vowel. It permits the word to be read, heard. When the point is missing, there is risk of gross misunder-

> standing. In fact, there is no such thing as a word. There are consonants waiting to become vocables.
>
> . . . the reader must himself recreate the word, which implies more than a profound comprehension, a true intuition of the text. At this stage, the reader joins the creator.

In an early poem, Edmond Jabès writes: "The sex is always a vowel." If we put these two quotes together, across time, we see two things. First, the word has a physical, sexual reality in addition to its intellectual and spiritual nature. Secondly, it is the reader/creator who reveals the sex of the word as he adds the vowel, who opens the word, not only as one opens a book, but as one opens a vulva. We have intercourse with words. With all the violence inherent in that term.

How much more violent, then, the process of breaking words apart, of playing in the breakage. To Marcel Cohen, Jabès calls it "a rape (*viol*) . . . of the untouchable Name of God." But it is a rape that proves futile, that does not establish any dominance over the words any more than writing does:

> The liberties taken with them open up an abyss: the abyss of the infinite possibilities offered by the handling of the letters, and of which we can ever only claim an arbitrary assemblage. That's why the word will always escape us.

But it may be that the word not only escapes us, but is itself destroyed:

> A slightly larger space within a word—the separation into syllables, for instance—an unexpected crack, a letter broken or dropped into the void give rise to such play within the word that it is drawn into a series of metamorphoses and destroyed in the process.

•

> If God is, it is because He is in the book. If sages, saints and prophets exist, if scholars and poets, men and insects exist, it is because their

names are found in the book. The world exists because the book does. For existing means growing with your name.

It is language, the book, that enables us to perceive—and to live. It is our universe to the point where we ourselves metamorphose into the word. "I took you in as a word," the narrator says to Yaël. And Jabès to Marcel Cohen: "We become the word that gives reality to the object, to the being." It is language, with its possibility of lies, of fiction. Truth, at least with a capital "T," is not for us. It is deadly like God, like silence, except where mediated through language. This is why truth, in time, is "the absurd and fertile quest of lies." And why, when the writer is about to drown in the ocean of the blank page, it is the word that allows him to swim, to stay on the surface.

Perhaps the word "has been given to us only so we could comfortably settle down in the lie." Or at least in that intermediate area of experiencing that is between subjective and objective, beyond true and false. The area D. W. Winnicott calls the "potential space between individual and environment," the area of playing, of cultural experience, art, religion, that makes available modes of paying attention to both external and internal experience. But comfortably? "I will tell you about the price he paid for lying, that is to say, for living."

•

Relation of walking and thinking, the movement of the body setting thought in motion. Rimbaud composed many of his poems while walking. So does Edmond Jabès. Walking the space of a line, a phrase. As if finding it. A grammar of motion.

•

Someone mentions "Yes, we have no bananas." Edmond's eyes light up:

"I remember that. That song was popular in Egypt, in the thirties." And he starts singing, suggesting music-hall routines till we roll on the floor.

•

Edmond Jabès does not write novels. Nor poems, for that matter. He claims to write in a new genre, "the book." Not even books. He writes *the* book that all his books are fragments of. As it in turn is an infinitesimal part of the The Book, the totality, the universe that never surrenders: *"Jamais le livre, dans son actualité, ne se livre."* At the same time, he tells Paul Auster, "The book carries all books within itself, and each fragment is the beginning of the book, the book that is created within the book and which at the same time is taken apart." Among the innumerable books that each book carries inside itself, some may come as a surprise:

> "What book do you mean?"
> "I mean the book within the book."
> "Is there another book hidden in what I read?"
> "The book you are writing."

The metaphor of the book does not seem to have one fixed meaning, but unfolds new aspects from one volume to the next. Most startling perhaps: "The invisible form of the book is the legible body of God." The two most frequent references for "the book" are writing and Judaism, but as Stéphane Mosès points out, neither is a key to the other. (In spite of the identification of writer and Jew.) And neither writing nor Judaism is a fixed or ready-made reality for Jabès, but one rather to be constantly reinvented.

While the book is a kind of totality Jabès does not see it as a closed system and never sets it, as Derrida does, in opposition to writing and its disruptive, aphoristic energy. Rather, the opposite of the book is the novel.

The novel, says Edmond Jabès, goes against the book because author and characters force themselves on the book and drown it in their voices. The "writer of the book" must sacrifice his voice to the book's own voice:

> Writing a book means joining your voice to the virtual voice of the margins. It means listening to the letters swimming in the ink like twenty-six blind fish before they are born for our eyes, that is to say, before they die fixed in their last cry of love. Then I shall have said what I had to say and what every page already knew. This is why the aphorism is the deepest expression of the book: it lets the margins breathe, it bears inside it the breath of the book and expresses the universe at the same time.

•

"What is given in an aphorism," Eric Gould comments, "is not exactly a subterfuge, but only a small part of what is really intended but not entirely known." The *Aphorisms* of Hippocrates opens this way:

> Life is short, art is long, opportunity fugitive, experimenting dangerous, reasoning difficult.

For my own sense of writing, the term "aphorism" implies still too much closure. Its etymology marks boundaries. It must, as Friedrich Schlegel said, "be complete in itself like a hedgehog," which Novalis seconded with: "The hedgehog—an ideal" and, more explicitly, "the greatest mass of thought in the smallest possible space." Though radiating outward like the spikes of the hedgehog?

Fragments, rather. Here, fragments of a lamentation, of a memoir of Edmond Jabès. Fragments about his work. About translation.

But with Jabès, too, the emphasis is not on isolating minimal units of meaning, but on the interruption, the gap between. "Interruption is one of the fundamental devices of all structuring," says Walter Benjamin. The shadow zone of silence, of margins, gains weight, becomes an element of structure. The interruption allows for breath, for possibility, for stopping to think.

And perspectivism. Inherent in the form of the fragment, it acknowledges the elusive whole, be it Jabès's transcendent totality or, for me, here, the man Edmond Jabès and his work. And encircles it at least to some degree, I hope.

"The fragment, the exploded book, is our only access to the infinite," Edmond Jabès says in conversation after conversation. And writes: "Only in fragments can we read the immeasurable totality."

Here he sees the difference between his concept of the book and Mallarmé's, with which his own is often associated (for instance, by Michel Leiris).

> Mallarmé wanted to put all knowledge into a book. . . . But in my opinion this book would be very ephemeral, since knowledge in itself is ephemeral. The book that would have a chance to survive, I think, is the book that destroys itself, that destroys itself in favor of another book that will prolong it. *(Interview with Paul Auster)*

The fragment as answer to system-building, as with the German Romantics? Where the system remains a challenge in the background, where fragmentation aims at surpassing and enlarging it to the point of the infinite where the infinitely small and the infinitely large fuse into one?

The fragment as approximation of the biblical technique that, according to Robert Alter, aims at producing a certain indeterminacy of meaning? "Meaning, perhaps for the first time in narrative literature, was conceived as a process, requiring continual revision . . . continual suspension of judgment, weighing of multiple possibilities, brooding over gaps in the information."

The fragment as enacting the Jewish tradition of interpretation as *"lire aux éclats,"* as exploding the text to safeguard its dynamics of "language in motion," in opposition to a Western ontology of presence?

Or as an attempt to settle between potential and act? To be and not be at the same time?

And is there a direct ratio: the more fragmented the closer to a totality, to potentiality? Susan Handelman believes that "for both Jabès and the rabbis, the very ambiguities, gaps, disruptions, uncertainties, and contradictions of scripture are the secret of its power."

I tend to think the fragment is our way of apprehending not just the infinite, but anything at all. Our inclusive views are all mosaics.

The shards catch light on the cut, the edges give off sparks. This is the case for Edmond Jabès as for Anne-Marie Albiach's *Etat*, where the fragmentation adds a charge of energy, even violence. A book I am reading in 1971, while working on *The Book of Questions*. And I hope that this is also happening in my *When They Have Senses*, which came out of this experience, its fragmentary syntax based on *Etat*, its texture fed, if less directly, by translating Jabès. I hope that the glimpses, as in Albiach and Jabès, amount to more than their sum, that they gain in intensity from allowing interruption, allowing possibility to enter. As Blanchot says:

> The sky is blue. Is the sky blue? Yes.
>
> The "Yes" does in no way reestablish the simplicity of the plain affirmation. In the question, the blue of the sky has given way to the void. The blue has, however, not dispersed, on the contrary it has risen dramatically to its POSSIBILITY, above its actual being. It unfolds in the intensity of this new space, bluer than it has ever been before.

•

I love David Mendelson's false etymology that derives the word "mosaic" from Moses, from his breaking of the tablets. This is certainly behind Jabès's "exploded book," where the death by scattering of God's word is the condition of legibility:

> By turning their back on the Tablets, the chosen people gave Moses a crucial lesson in reading. From instinct—for is the Book not prior to man?—they raised the rape of God to the level of original death. And, rising up against the letter, their independence consecrated the fracture in which God writes Himself against God.
>
> The destroyed book allows us to read the book.

Blanchot puts his finger on another reason why this breaking of the Tablets haunts Jabès. It means that there is no "original word," no unbroken relation with the divine:

> The Tablets of the Law were broken when still only barely touched by the divine hand . . . and were written again, but not in their original form, so that it is from an already destroyed word that man learns

> the demand that must speak to him: there is no real first understanding, no initial and unbroken word, as if one could never speak except the second time, after having refused to listen and having taken a distance in regard to the origin.

Jabès knows this. In "Adam, or the Birth of Anxiety," he places the break even earlier in the Biblical myth:

> And God created Adam.
> He created him a man, depriving him of memory.
> Man without childhood, without past.
> (Without tears, without laughter or smiles.)
> Man come out of Nothing, unable even to claim a portion of this Nothing.

He also knows that it is the absence of a divine word that allows *us* to speak in addition to reading, allows us eloquence:

> Reb Jacob also believed in eloquence. He compared it to a stone tearing the surface of a lake and to its misleading rings. The wound closes right up again. But the rings multiply and grow and bear witness—O mockery—to the intensity of the pain.
>
> The divine utterance is silenced as soon as it is pronounced. But we cling to its resonant rings, our inspired words.
>
> Eloquence is created by the absence of a divine word.
>
> It is at the beginning of speech. We are crushed by the deity. The echo dies as the voice weakens. The murmur is truly human.

Behind Jabès's "exploded book," there obviously stands the dispersion of the Jewish people, the continual scattering that is the Jewish experience. Also the Kabbalistic tradition of the Breaking of the Vessels, of which I know too little. The "light of the first day" was too intense for the finite "vessels" of the world. The divine emanations could not properly relate to each other or be received. The vessels burst, and the light dispersed into innumerable sparks. "In every word shine multiple lights," says the Zohar. And Susan Handelman:

> Thus in Kabbalah, it is not only the tablets of the law that are broken. The universe itself has undergone a primordial shattering; God has withdrawn; the Vessels are broken; the divine sparks are lost in the material world. As Scholem reads it, Kabbalah is a great myth of exile.

Edmond Jabès reenacts this process on the level of the alphabet:

> To fragment the name of God, which is formed of all the words in the language, to reduce it to a single word, single syllable, single letter. So, at the end of the night, we approached the alphabet.
>
> To reassemble the scattered pieces in their new relation, into the exemplary Tables.

•

> The fragment is not a particular style or failure, it is the very form of the written. . . . First of all, the caesura lets the meaning rise. Not by itself, of course; but without the interruption—between the letters, words, sentences, books—no meaning could awaken. *Assuming* that Nature refuses *leaps,* we understand why Writing will never be Nature. It proceeds only by leaps. *(Jacques Derrida)*

The spark given off by the edges of the shards, the fragments, is the stronger the more abrupt the cut, the more strongly it makes us feel the lack of transition, the more disparate the surrounding texts. This latter is true of most figures of speech, certainly of the two elements of metaphor, as Reverdy, for instance, has pointed out. It may be fruitful to examine in terms of metaphor the texts Jabès juxtaposes across white space.

When the linearity of reading is broken, when we are startled awake, when the smooth horizontal travel of eye/mind is interrupted, when the connection is broken, there is a kind of orchestral meaning that comes about in the leap. A vertical dimension vibrating with the energy field between the two lines (phrases, sentences), and perhaps the energy of what would have followed/preceded, but is lacking. A meaning that both illuminates the separation and connects across it. A meaning that goes beyond the two elements that border it, as metaphor goes beyond the sum of tenor and vehicle.

Maybe the power of the leap is simply that it cuts out explanation, an essential act of poetry (and of philosophy, Wittgenstein would say).

But for Blanchot, discontinuity is more than this. It is "the breathing of discourse" and "the mystery of language itself":

> [Interruption] carries the mystery of language itself: pause between phrases, pause from one speaker to the other, and pause of attention, of understanding which doubles the power of expression . . . pause which, alone, makes speech into conversation and even into speech. . . . The gap, the discontinuity assures continuity of understanding. . . . It is the breathing of discourse. . . .
>
> But there is another kind of interruption. It introduces waiting, which measures the distance between two speakers, not the reducible distance, but the irreducible. . . . Now what is at stake is the strangeness between us. . . .

This last paragraph applies equally to translation, whose ultimate task may be to bear witness to the *essentially* irreducible strangeness and distance between languages—but whose immediate task is exactly to explore this space.

•

A friendship across distance and time. Two almost-years in Paris, in 1971 and 1983/4, the summer months of 1973, 1975, 1976, 1979, 1988. In the U.S., three to five weeks each time in 1976, 1978, 1981, 1983, 1986. And in Paris again, for the last time, in May 1989, at the celebration for Edmond's seventy-seventh birthday.

Edmond Jabès dies in January 1991; Arlette Jabès in August 1992.

" 'It is not only a word you form in writing, you also delimit a moment of your life,' he had noted." The matter of words, the matter of your life. Precarious life since the sign by definition makes common cause with death. Which is why Hegel called language divine: "not because it eternalizes what it names, but because it overthrows what it names and changes it into something else." It cannot name without separating the object from its materiality.

"Logic can take care of itself," says Wittgenstein. But the body?

•

A student asks what sustained me in translating so many volumes of Jabès. I say: Envy and pleasure in destruction.

I am not altogether joking. Destruction is unavoidable. Sound, sense, form, reference will never again stand in the same relation to each other. I have to break apart this "seemingly natural fusion" of elements, melt it down to—what? The "genetic code" of the work I have called it, following Novalis who contrasts a superficial "symptomatic imitation" with "genetic imitation." It is a state in which the finished work is dissolved back into a state of fluidity, of potential, of "molten lava" (Haroldo de Campos)—not unlike the "state of dissolution" in which "reality is contained in language," according to Wilhelm von Humboldt. In this state, the translator will be able, with a mix of imagination and understanding, to penetrate into the work and re-create it.

There is pleasure in the destruction because it makes the work mine. It is the same "no" to what already exists that is a crucial part of all making, even making a translation. Destruction is part of creation. It provides the energy.

Envy provides the impulse. August Wilhelm Schlegel admits: "I cannot look at my neighbor's poetry without immediately coveting it with all my heart, so that I am the prisoner of continuous poetical adultery." Just so have I loved and coveted Jabès's work. A work so rich in pleasures, with such scope, such depth that it has fed my own thinking endlessly, has taken me into metaphysical dimensions that are not in my own "nature." How could I not want to have written it?

Together, I say, these two vices have allowed me to write a work that I could never have written on my own.

The student replies: You mean it allowed you to *read* this work—and suddenly we are at the heart of Jabès's work. For him, we write only what we have been allowed to read, what we must interpret. And it is little. The book of the universe never surrenders:

> We can only write what we have been given to read. It is an infinitesimal part of the universe to be told. The book in its actual state never surrenders.

Neither does Jabès's text.

•

The story is not given. God does not exist. The center is empty. The real world, the "book" of the universe, is undecipherable.

"Our lot is to interpret an unreadable world."

"In the beginning is hermeneutics," repeats Jacques Derrida.

Interpretation. Commentary. The central procedure of *The Book of Questions*. Even in the later volumes, which do not have a story to comment on, the structure remains commentary: on words, on aphorisms, on the stories of the earlier volumes, on the earlier volumes themselves.

> "In the word *commentaire*," he repeated, "there are the words *taire, se taire, faire taire,* 'to be silent, to fall silent, to silence,' which quotation demands."

Commentaire. Comment taire. Edmond Jabès's "commentary" teaches us how to be silent. Our English *commentary* at best *tarries*. Which is banal. With its paradoxical incongruity, Jabès's *comment taire*, "how to be silent, to fall silent, to silence," jolts us into thinking. It astonishes and opens new perspectives.

Jabès's own comments on this text begin with common sense:

> To comment on something is, in effect, to reduce to silence an already established and fixed meaning. But it also means to reduce to silence

> the immediate perception we have of the text so as to give it a chance to speak by itself.

But they quickly crescendo to speculation: "It is not the commentary comments, but the text that inspired it. Commentary is dumb."

A hope that commentary, which is within our possibilities, will end up making the essential text, the silence, speak through it? A way of acknowledging that we do not create ex nihilo, that there is always a previous text? That language, which is our world, does "contain the objects of reality," as Wilhelm von Humboldt says, but in a state of dissolution, "as it were dissolved into ideas," accessible to us only *as text,* as something to be interpreted, commented?

And later: we comment because we cannot bear the silences in the book, which are, lastly, the silence of God. "Every commentary is first of all a commentary on a silence."

As far as we can imagine an end to the infinite regress of text behind text, it must be silence. Later, in *El, or the Last Book*, Edmond Jabès has *comment taire* lead, via its sound, to *comment être*, how to be. For how could we bear silence, creatures of language that we are? How could our exercises in discourse overcome discourse? Could they contain their own limits? A silent commentary on an original silence? The essential text is the divine silence, the unpronounceable Name, symbol of a symbol, inaccessibility to the second power, which is also the illegible that lies in wait back where legibilty falters.

> In the beginning is hermeneutics. But this *shared* impossibility of joining the *center* of the sacred text and this *shared* need for exegesis is interpreted differently by the poet and the rabbi . . . the original opening to interpretation means essentially that henceforward there will always be rabbis and poets. And two interpretations of interpretation. Then Law turns into Question, and the right to speak fuses with the duty to interrogate. The book of man is a book of questions. *(Jacques Derrida)*

The key word here is "opening," which Ouaknin, too, sees as the essence of commentary "in the sense of the expression of Midrash and Zohar, *Patah véamar:* 'He opened and said,' 'he broke the verse open and said.' " The "sacred text" or Jabès's "universe" are not given as immutable orthodoxy, but are open to interpretation, opened up by commentary. Which means they lastly owe their existence to it. Through it they are alive, changing, are language in motion.

Susan Handelman gives the same importance to the opening that is interpretation, but she seems to see less difference between the rabbi's and the poet's:

> Even in "normative" Judaism, the opening of interpretation is extraordinary. . . . The rabbinical word remains ever open, unfulfilled, in process. Yet there is great risk here; this inner dynamic accounts for both the creativity of Judaism and its own inversions and undoing. Where is the line between interpretation and subversion? I have elsewhere called this a "heretic hermeneutic," which is a complex of identification with the Text and its displacement. Jabès's book is precisely this identification with the Sacred Book and its displacement. The Book is now opened to include even its own inversions.

"The Jew has for centuries questioned his truth which has become the truth of questioning," says Edmond Jabès.

•

Commentary. This means that. This is that. "The pages of the book are doors. . . . The soul is a moment of light. . . . Distance is light." Nouns and nouns. The nouns dominate, as they tend to in French. *(Je suis dans l'impossibilité de venir!)* The verbs are rarer, especially in the aphorisms. Not absent like the story, but almost.

In English, the "this is that" pattern can get monotonous. I feel I have to turn nouns into verbs—or adjectives—where I can: *Voir, c'est la traversée des miroirs* into "to see is to go through mirrors" (with of course a loss of rhyme); *la découverte de l'ouvrage qu'il écrira* into "discovering the work he will write"; *dans l'agitation des ombres amoureuses* into "when lovers' shadows move"; *la perennité des tables* into "the perennial tablets"; etc.

Along with too many nouns, there are too many copulas, too many "is" and "are" for my ears when I translate word for word. If the context permits I cut. "God: an endless word" for *Dieu est un mot sans fin*. True, this makes for a somewhat more elliptical style than Jabès's, whose syntax is very classical. However, there are enough passages where Jabès leaves out the copula that I feel justified in doing it just a bit more often.

D'un mot a un mot,	From one word to another,
vide possible,	possible void,
au loin,	far,
irresistible.	irresistible.
Le rêve en est l'acompte;	Dream the instalment,
le petit, le premier	the small,
acompte.	the first one down.

Have I betrayed you? I have certainly betrayed you. But I move with the muscle of English that moves with its verbs where French revels in nouns, proper for propositions, for logic.

•

When I say I make Jabès's work "mine," I do not at all mean adapting him to "my style." On the contrary, I want to "write Jabès" in English, write *à l'écoute de* Jabès, write listening to his French.

My translation process always moves through three stages—I should say four, actually, because there is of course a preliminary stage of intense reading, which, together with my first round of writing (interlinear, almost word for word) attempts to understand the work. Antoine Berman is right that a translator's understanding is "different from a hermeneutico-critical comprehension." It aims more at retracing the author's steps, his creative process, than at analyzing how the finished product fits within its culture. As Valéry puts it:

> Translating . . . makes us try to step into the vestiges of the author's footprints; not to fashion one text out of another, but to go back from

> this one to the virtual epoch of its formation, to the phase where the state of mind is that of an orchestra whose instruments awaken, call out to one another, try to be in tune before the concert.

In the second round, I do not look at the French. I must separate myself from its authority. I treat the mess of the first draft (which is neither French nor quite English) as if it were a draft of my own, though with a sense of the text's intentionality in mind. I try to reproduce, re-create it in English. The importance of this stage of separation cannot be exaggerated, and I am still grateful that I was very early pointed in this direction by Justin O'Brien.

In the third round, I go back to dialogue with the French and try to wrestle the English as close to the French as possible.

It is hard to say if one stage is more important than another. Each is only possible once I have gone through the preceding one. I can only write an English text once I have "understood" the French. I can only get close to the French once I have a text that can stand by itself as a text in English. With Jabès, much of the work at the third stage has been on syntax, on letting the sentences approach again the length of the French ones, on trying to catch the rhythm of the paragraphs.

My (and Justin O'Brien's) three stages of the translation process correspond more or less to the three stages of translation that Goethe saw following one another in history: the first is simple and prosaic (*schlicht-prosaisch*) and wants to know what a work "says."

The second, which he calls "parodistic," adapts the foreign work's spirit to our own culture. This stage, which Goethe assigns to the early eighteenth century and especially to the French, is still the dominant mode in English-speaking countries, as Lawrence Venuti has shown. Translation of this kind is praised as "transparent" or "seamless." It reflects the values of our science-dominated culture by "valorizing a purely instrumental use of language and . . . immediate intelligibility." Looked at from a political angle, it appears less harmless than "parodistic" would indicate: at the very least it domesticates, at worst it is imperialist and colonizing.

In Goethe's third and highest stage, finally, the translator tries to make his work identical with the original. This at first encounters resistance among readers because a translator who "attaches himself so closely to his original more or less abandons the originality of his own nation. The result is a third [term] toward which the taste of the public must first be educated."

This "third" is of the greatest interest. It is important that, in contrast to the domesticating, colonizing model, this translation follows the foreign work so closely it almost abandons its own language and culture. It is, in Schleiermacher's phrase, "towards a foreign likeness bent." Hence Venuti calls it "foreignizing." Its locus is definitely new ground somewhere between the two languages, perhaps overlapping both. A border region, Hocquard's "blank spot" on the map.

I part company with Goethe when he goes on to say that the last, the translation that tries to identify with the original, in the end, tends to approach the interlinear and thus close the circle. This owes more to Goethe's love of circular patterns than to an understanding of translation.

But it is no doubt one source of the value Walter Benjamin places (at least in theory) on literal word-by-word rendering of syntax—which has served as justification for much "translatorese" I see as editor of a translation series. I am not talking here about radically "literal" projects in the wake of Celia and Louis Zukofsky's monumental *Catullus* that, by focusing on the materiality of a foreign text, enrich the possibilities of our language (I will come back to this). I am talking about translators whose ear is no match for their theoretical sophistication, and who produce work that, under pretext of cultivating strangeness, has not gotten beyond what I consider the first stage of the process. For the practice of translation, Venuti's and Schleiermacher's concept of "foreignizing" seems more valuable to me than Benjamin's word-by-word because it directs attention to the whole foreign work and its context, rather than to, or in addition to, the single word.

Curiously, Benjamin combines advocating word-by-word, which would seem to value the materiality of a text, with an utterly abstract, Hegelian view of translation as *progress* toward "a higher and purer linguistic air," a step closer to "pure language." (Clearly these are his terms for Goethe's "third," for Hocquard's "blank spot," for the border region between languages that translation aims at—though I would hardly call it "higher.") Benjamin's "progress" owes much to Novalis's equally Hegelian sense of translation as "potentialization": no work can ever quite come up to its idea, to what it ideally wants to be. Translation separates it from its first empirical embodiment and is therefore necessarily closer to the idea. True, only the highest kind of translation, the "mythical" translation, achieves this, not the lowlier "grammatical" and "changing" (*verändernd*) versions, which are closely patterned on Goethe's "prosaic" and "parodistic" stages. Novalis's third kind, the "mythic translation," however, departs radically from Goethe's in that "it does not give us the actual work of art, but its ideal." In this spirit, Novalis could write to A. W. Schlegel, "I am convinced the German Shakespeare now is better than the English one."

Neither Novalis nor Benjamin seem to think about the fact that translation cannot stay on the level of the "idea," but must *re-embody* it in the second particular language, as concretely and bodily as in the first.

•

Edmond Jabès walks. Hands crossed in back. Slowly.

•

7, rue de l'Epée de Bois. Street of the Wooden Sword. Coincidence? The theater lover is delighted and amused. Though he also laments it as the writer's (and hospitality's) insufficient defence against the hostility of men: "a ridiculous wooden sword against the viril sword of the duel." Yet his preference is clear. And he knows that even such a sword, even hitting out at the void, will draw blood—though it will be the writer's own.

> "A saber stroke in the void, this is the image of my life and writing I would like to leave behind," he said. "And if drops of my blood

> have more than once soiled the ground, you must understand that each of them is an unknown book."

The building is at the corner of the Street of the Patriarchs. Coincidence?

Two flights up. The door to the salon is diagonally across from the French window onto the balcony. An arc of in and out, inviting the outside to enter into the space of a room, but also to leave again.

Out of this window, what does Edmond Jabès see?

The house across, with its more intricate ironwork, with two large stone flowers on the facade. His street, which

> is prodigious in that it partakes of all the streets in the world. Yet it is short and narrow. The building in its middle houses the post office. There it suffers a change which opens it to the five continents.

No wonder that he finds the word *rue* inserted into *universe*. But mostly, he sees beyond the street and the city all the way to the desert, the non-place he claims as his own.

His time. He would scoff: who can know what his time is?

The present joining the past even as he looks at it.

The past, done and finished. But he looks at its traces. Dark. He knows what that is.

The future, which he hopes will be a little brighter—better for the questioning, the urgent questioning—and fears it will not.

Visitors sit on the green sofa facing the desk and a painting by Angelopoulos. A cityscape, hundreds of doors that seem less to lead into houses than into a space of loneliness, pale gray-green-blue like sky or ocean, with one lone figure—a traveler, a transient, definitely not at home. To the right, a glassed-in case that holds Edmond Jabès's most treasured books, with letters, postcards stuck in, photos, pebbles placed in front. And small drawings. To the left the balcony door. Left of that, a blond wood sculpture, waist high, by cousin Piera Rossi. Rounded forms, female, but with a torque. Torque of torment, says Edmond. Behind it and behind the sofa, bookshelves stuffed, overflowing. Edmond's armchair off to the right, between a cabinet carrying two Chinese jade figures and, on the other side, over the heating, his head in bronze by the Japanese sculptor, Kono. Without chin. Edmond reenacts his stupor when the sculptor declared: *Je vous coupe le menton.* (And he has a strong one!) Around his armchair, piles of books, new arrivals, on the floor. Above, on the wall, Francesca Chandon's square etched white on white.

And Arlette. The room comes alive as she enters. Even in 1984, when she is having radiation treatments. She feels exhausted, she says, but seems bubbling with energy. Edmond more tired. Pale. Eyes returning to his face as if from a distance. But still bringing the extraordinary blue of a Mediterranean sky with them.

When we visit Arlette after Edmond's death his voice still seems to hang in the room. Grave, then dissolving into laughter.

•

In the dining room, Edmond opens a drawer full of pebbles he has collected on beaches. In Brittany. In Italy.

"Look at this, wouldn't you say, a face? And this one here, magnificent."

Almost all his pebbles have markings one could see as a face.

"Just look: it's Verlaine."

Once he has said this I cannot see anything but Verlaine in the veins of the stone. But I think more of how it is sand and stone that hold his attention rather than the sea. Bits of desert. And how his obsession with faces must come out of—must be a reaction against—the taboo on representation in Judaism. Taboo that weighs most heavily on the face.

Jacqueline Chaillet and Marcel Cohen vacation with the Jabèses in Brittany. Jacqueline and Arlette lie in their beach chairs and worship the sun. Whenever they look up they see Marcel and Edmond walking along the beach, bent over, scrutinizing the sand. Back at the hotel, Edmond is the first to spread out his treasures.

"Look, Marcel, isn't this incredible? Look at this face, and that one's glorious, would you believe it is not the work of an artist?"

Marcel hmms, not overly taken. Then shows *his* finds which are the opposite of Edmond's. He is after perfection of shape, markings that approach the geometrical.

Edmond hmms and returns to his faces.

After Edmond's death Marcel gives us a most precious gift. Two out of a group of five white pebbles that Edmond has collected for him. These do not suggest faces. They are pure white. They are, strangely, almost perfect cubes. They sit on top of one another.

•

"Involution." With this word Gabriel Bounoure describes the movement of the first trilogy, *The Book of Questions, The Book of Yukel, Return to the Book*. Involution rather than dialectic. A circular process connecting accident and law, particulars and forces. With an emphasis on process, on *errance* (errantry, wandering) at the risk of getting lost: "as if accepting diachrony would one day lead to another dimension, to a synchrony incorporated in the book." A process that begins and ends with the infinite, but goes through the earth with its kingdom of love, its nightmare of history, on to the book and the word, our bridge back to the unnamable and infinite.

The following three books, *Yaël, Elya, Aely,* vary the same process with a different, more allegorical story about the interaction of writer and word. From the silence of a still-born child to the struggle of lovers (writer and word) for life in the book, and back to death, its law in life and in the book.

Then, with *El, or the Last Book*, the group of seven complicates the triadic structure. But this seventh book again, in one volume, follows the pattern of involution. It is a meditation on the point as God's first manifestation, which expanded to encompass all of creation, and to which all creation returns. If this seems to hold out hope of an ultimate unification, Jabès suggests that it is at the price of existence. ("Point," in French, also is the full stop, the period, and a strong negative.)

Next, another trilogy: *The Book of Resemblances*. It marks a further turn of involution in that it uses *The Book of Questions* as the basis for its meditations in the way the latter had used the story of the lovers deported by the Nazis. This "book which resembles a book" probes the nature of analogy, which is at the root of thought and language, yet proves to be a tenuous support for man created in the image of a god who does not exist. In these books, man is exiled even from his own myths and metaphysical origin. He resembles nothing.

And finally four more, meant to be gathered into *The Book of Limits (The Little Book of Unsuspected Subversion, The Book of Dialogue, Le parcours* [The Itinerary], *The Book of Shares)* to form another seven. Not counting the posthumous *Livre de l'hospitalité* and various smaller works, like *The Book of Margins*.

Always circling around an unreachable center. Two centers, rather: the "spiritual" one that we might call God, meaning, silence, and the "lower" one that is the scream, the open wound—likewise out of the reach of language. Spiraling course, open-ended, beginning and ending with the infinite, but intersecting all the planes of history, geography, society, culture.

And do not think Jabès missed the "center" contained in "concentration." The Camp as a grotesque historical parody of the center, which is always out of reach.

Fall and redemption? No, I don't see that. Not Bounoure's "guérison par le livre" either. Not that Bounoure dares fully hope for a healing through the book himself. The values are more ambiguous. An image of illogic and paradox perhaps: if the beginning is the same as the end, causality and time are eliminated, replaced by the mirror.

Questions that do not engender the answers they intend, but lead to more questions, perpetuating their own form. The questions, too, are mirrors. There are no answers, only questions.

Is this the world of Jabès's books only? Listen to a scientist:

> We are condemned to live in a world where every question opens another, and that to infinity. . . . I am afraid that all those who still

> aspire to synthesis or unity are wishfully calling for a time that is past. I am afraid they will obtain this synthesis only at the price of either tyranny or renunciation. *(Robert Oppenheimer)*

And, to paraphrase Marcel Cohen: that part of our literature that is conscious of itself and its time knows that it has been deprived of its power of synthesis, that if it maintains the appearance of coherence, of meaning, of destiny, it only tries to reanimate phantoms.

Does this imply that there is no creation, only reflection? No beings, only images? "We write only what we have been allowed to read."

"But," counters Daniel Accursi, revising Nietzsche, "the spiral is the Eternal Return—not of the Same, but of the Other, not of the identical, but of difference. The eternal return of difference explains the unforeseeable creativity of time."

I try to follow this lead. I circle among Jabès's books. Among my memories of him, Keith's memories of him. I repeat lines so that different contexts might open different perspectives. I try to circle, encircle, Edmond Jabès.

•

> A young disciple asks his master, "If you never give me an answer, how shall I know that you are the master and I the disciple?" And the master responds, "By the order of the questions."
>
> *(Interview with Jason Weiss)*

So it is syntax that makes the difference. Arrangement. Composition.

As Gertrude Stein says: "Everything is the same except composition and as the composition is different and always going to be different everything is not the same." And Mary Carruthers moves composition into what seems a single thought:

> *Cogitatio* (*con +agito*, "move, rouse") is defined in rhetoric as a combinative or compositional activity of the mind. It necessarily uses

memory because it combines *imagines* from memory's store. One should therefore think of a single *cogitatio* or "thought" as a small-scale composition, a bringing together (*con+pono*) of various "bits" (*phantasmata*) in one's inventory.

•

Edmond has bought an edition of the Koran. Three paperback volumes in a box. He is handling the books—and especially the box, the *coffret*—with obvious pleasure.

"This is how I would like *The Book of Questions*."

Keith teases: "You would like *The Book of Questions* to be the Koran?"

Edmond is brought up short for a moment, then bursts into laughter:

"Yes. My Book of the Book is *The Book of Questions*!"

But the gestures are lacking, the expression on his face, the sound of the laugh. And already it's all wrong.

•

It must have been in 1979, before the summer we spend with Edmond and Arlette, that Edmond refuses a bypass. He opts for the alternative, a completely salt-free diet. But not without sending his cardiologist a quote from *The Book of Job:* "Can that which is unsavoury be eaten without salt? or is there any taste in the white of an egg?" The doctor does not think it funny.

In the following months, Arlette, meaning to help Edmond, shares his diet—and gets ill. Her blood pressure has dropped dangerously. Not you, says the doctor.

In spite of long preparation, or perhaps because of it, Edmond Jabès's death, on January 2, 1991, comes as a shock.

Edmond's father, when he got around to going to city hall, mistakenly declared Edmond's birth as April 14, 1912, two days before he was actually born.

One of the first obituaries puts his death two days late, January 4, 1991, rather than January 2.

What would Edmond have made of this symmetry? He thought of the two prenatal days as lived in death (*Néant, né en,* he identifies. "It is nothingness we are born in.") Where was he the two days post mortem?

The two "prenatal" days haunt him, give him the sense of death, absence, emptiness that is at the heart of his books. He writes about them twice, in *Elya* and in *Intimations The Desert*:

> Is it to this error in calculation I unconsciously owe the feeling that I have always been separated from my life by forty-eight hours? The two days added to mine could only be lived in death.
>
> As with the book, as with God in the world, the first manifestation of my existence was an absence which bore my name.

> In any case, this error in calculation, which I would never consider as such, but rather as a chance warning, distressed me so much that I made up my own explanation. I saw it as concrete proof furnished by the unconscious that *we are older than our life*. Out of this guaranteed void, this countersigned outside-of-time, *The Book of Questions* has drawn its voice and place . . .

•

Yet when I am working on a novel, *The Hanky of Pippin's Daughter,* and toy with making it epistolary, Edmond warns me off: "Letters—that makes two absences."

•

In *Sous la Coupole*, Jean Daive speaks of *arrière-absence*.

I like all the *arrière, ante-, avant-* Edmond Jabès places at the beginnings of his books. In the first books it's only an *Avant-dire*. It is not simply "preface" or "foreword." Something spoken, not written, before the actual space of the book. A "Fore-speech" for lack of anything more elegant, followed by a "Threshold." Later, more and more delays, preparations, approaches before we reach the actual "Book." Which is often much shorter than the preliminary sections. "All this 'fore-speech' hangs over the book in order to negate it," says Gabriel Bounoure.

Ante-Thresholds and Ante-Ante-Thresholds.

Still later, the Thresholds, Doors, Walls, Roofs disappear. It is no longer certain we are approaching a dwelling. The spaces we wander through become: "The Time Before the Story," *L'arrière-livre*, (The Ground of the Book), a space "Before the Fore-Book," the "Fore-Book," or simply "Approaches."

More and more difficult, the approach. The writer less and less sure he can reach the book, precarious place. He is only sure of the labor of the road. The reader both taken by the hand in welcome and warned: the book may not be for you.

Hesitation before encounter, terror of the unknown, the blank page, the Book.

"The threshold is perhaps death." Like any beginning.

But also the desire to keep the initial, inchoate material "as long as possible in a state of chaos at the book's very threshold, so that the reader too may witness the birth of the work."

It is the *Arrière-livre* in *Elya* that proves most difficult to translate. The dictionary lists:

> *Arrière:* behind, back, rear; *arrière-saison*, late autumn; *arrière-bouche*, back of the mouth; *arrière-garde*, rear-guard; *arrière-gout*, aftertaste; *arrière-grandmère*, great-grandmother; *arrière-main*, back of the hand; *arrière-pensée*, mental reservation, dissembled thought, ulterior motive; *arrière-plan*, background; *arrière-scène*, backstage . . .

I finally settle for "The Ground of the Book" and "Approaching the Ground of the Book."

Arrière-absence.

•

Not only the approach of the book becomes more and more difficult. The writer seems less and less sure of what he is saying. We go from one "perhaps" to the next. More and more sentences begin with "What if" or "And if." In the later volumes, the subjunctive seems almost the main mood.

I am very aware of this because my ear resists many "would" 's in a row. The sentences would (!) become heavy, the rhythm professorial. But in the indicative, how keep the stance of speculation from turning into assertion, into a tone of authority, which is exactly what Jabès's mood negates? I again decide each case as it comes up, varying with "perhaps," "possibly," "could it be that," . . .

I thought that the subjunctive began to dominate in *Yaël* and *Elya*. After all, Yaël is the personification of the word with its/her possibility of lies, its/her lack of reality, of "ontic density," as Gabriel Bounoure says. And if we do not know whether she is alive or dead at the end, Elya, her child, is definitely still-born. So there are many sentences like:

> Yesterday, Elya would have been ten years old.
>
> O Yaël, how I would have loved you. . . . You would have been mine down to your very soul. . . .
> I would say: "Yaël . . ." as if I were still speaking to her . . . "I would have liked to help you, Yaël, because that way I would have acted in keeping with my soul. . . ."

But these sentences are a matter of specific situations. The subjunctive as speculative mode comes to dominate later and more gradually. By the time we get to *The Book of Shares*, its presence is constant. It brings with it an increase in abstraction, an intensification of speculation, thought pushing ever more boldly—if ever more tentatively—into possibility:

"What if the word lied not only to man, but to God also? Our idea of truth would be seriously shaken," he said.

What if Eve's sin were really the sin of God which Eve, for love of Him, took on herself?

•

In back of the book: it is Keith who first picks up a book by Edmond Jabès, *Je bâtis ma demeure*. A short poem he translates is the first Jabès to be published in English. Later he translates a substantial selection of this book and of *Des deux mains* under the title *If There Were Anywhere but Desert*. This "Selected Poems" had been commissioned by the Jewish Publication Society. When Keith sends in the manuscript there is no response for a long time. Finally, a letter: the publisher will not publish the book. Keith calls and asks, why? It seems the poems are not Jewish enough.

Station Hill Press makes a beautiful book of it.

•

There is no picture of the desert in Edmond Jabès's apartment. He does not need it. He carries the desert inside himself.

"Would you like to go back to Egypt? Revisit the desert?"

"Non. Le désert m'a foutu à la porte."

I love this answer: The desert kicked me out, yes, but "out the door"! Elsewhere, Edmond states that the break with Egypt was a kind of relief because it brought the condition of exile out into the open or, rather, it revealed to him that his destiny was part of the collective Jewish destiny of exile.

At the time of the Suez crisis, in December 1956, when Jews were kicked out of Egypt, when Edmond Jabès came to France, Keith and I were trying to hitchhike in the South of France. We wondered why the roads were so empty. Until a medical doctor, entitled to a bit of gasoline, gave us a ride and explained.

In 1994, Irving Petlin draws a series of pastels based on *The Book of Questions*. With fine intuition, he translates the desert into a desert of Paris roofs.

> This morning between rue Monge and la Mouffe (after the rue des Patriarches and rue de l'Epée-de-Bois where I live) I let the desert invade my neighborhood. The Nile was not far.

"It is a space at once full and empty, sounding and silent," Michael Palmer describes Petlin's series, and:

> There is a brooding, darker character to the large work, a sea of flickering, rooftop details creating at once a multiplicity of signs and a void . . . It is a work that, like many of Petlin's, brings into question the boundary between the abstract and the representational through its sense of field and pattern.

•

Writing: to find a path in the desert, in uncharted territory.

On the one hand, the desert, image of dispersion, and on the other, the unreachable center: these are the two foci of Jabès's elliptical thought.

When Yukel drives into the desert he is intoxicated by the grandiose space, but it brings him face to face with death in a sandstorm:

> At noon, he found himself facing the infinite, the blank page. All tracks, footprints, paths were gone. Buried.

The infinite, the unnamable that writing intends is there, always, ready to destroy: "Whatever escapes us destroys us."

Impossible topography of writing. The infinite is both the center we try to encircle with a multitude of words, things, experiences, and is also outside, surrounding us. It is both condition and aim. But where is the infinite unless in our consciousness of possibility? Do we not create what destroys us? Even death? "The animals look out into the open," says Rilke. They do not see death. And their world before words is one of the frontiers, one of the limits of language that Edmond Jabès's words push toward.

> The Real, which is the sand, and the Nothing, which is the sky, are my two horizons.

The paths are there, on the page, already buried before they are traced. The ones we find are, of course, not straight, but circuitous. The longest may turn out the shortest. They often seem to lead away from the goal, in circles.

When one rabbi complains that their arguments have gone in circles like horses in an arena, Reb Acher replies:

> The tree goes in rings to its full height, and the bee around its honey-probe. Did not Reb Azar write: "The road of knowledge is rounder than an apple?"

Circling, spiraling, is the organic way, the way of the imagination. In a paradoxical space where in is out, and the beginning is the end, the straight line is as inadequate as the logic of two times two equals four. The latter, it is true, rules the earth and tends to find both Jews and writers expendable,

> for we hold that 2 times 2 equals also 5, or 7, or 9 . . . for we are the torment of logic. In the addition of even numbers, we are the order and disorder of the uneven figure.

•

Edmond speaks of the library he had to leave behind, in Egypt. This is what he regrets most. The loss of his property, he says, is compensated for by his having been able to leave a métier he detested. But he misses his classics and does not have the heart to replace them. He mourns his first editions, his treasures, Max Jacob's books, above all.

He discovered Jacob through Cocteau's *Rappel à l'ordre,* around 1930, entered into correspondence with him and, as Didier Cahen records, in 1933 gave a lecture on Jacob's work that got him the reputation of being a madman. Edmond loves to tell of his pilgrimage to Max Jacob in 1935, when he and Arlette were spending their honeymoon in Paris. Jacob's legendary red dressing gown, his little apartment full of posters, prints, and books. Jacob was most cordial, even offered the familiar *tu*. But after Edmond showed him his manuscript Jacob recommended he tear it up, "so that they could speak more freely about it." Edmond could not believe his ears. He protested, incredulous. Then Jacob went through the poems: "This is beautiful, but it isn't you. This is interesting, but it is Eluard. This here, Musset. A lot of it is more Max Jacob than Edmond Jabès. . . ." Edmond went home, burned the manuscript and wrote to Jacob: "I have given my poems a splendid funeral."

(Leiris's biographer, Aliette Armel, points out that Max Jacob was always tough on his young disciples. He for instance wrote to Kahnweiler, "Young Michel Leiris is becoming a true poet," while taking care not to say so to Leiris directly.)

In *From the Desert to the Book*, Edmond describes the scene differently: Jacob tears up the manuscript in his presence. Slip of memory? Two different occasions? No matter. What matters is the lesson that "all true closeness goes through difference."

"It took Max Jacob to cure me of my false romanticism," Edmond tells me. "I started writing very young. I was handed around the Parisian salons as a prodigy when I was fifteen. I wore a beautiful red bow tie. And my wretched juvenile poems were recited by an actor of the Comédie Française! I even met Maeterlinck, who was by then extremely old."

And there are Jacob's letters. If Edmond expected Jacob to advocate giving free rein to the imagination, he was disappointed. Jacob advises to condense, to resist an easy flow, to work toward rigorous form, rigorous syntax.

> I think poetry as "game" has had its day, and we need poets both wide-awake and serious. . . . I am happy to appreciate your spirit, your passion, your passionate spirit, but a cry is not a work. I fear *mots en liberté* is a bit old-fashioned. . . . [H]ow about trying to put all this in sentences-syntaxes!

On other occasions, on the contrary, Jacob finds Edmond's texts "too tight," "too laconic"—"Read Chateaubriand for his sentences." Or again "too lyrical"—"Read the classics to learn modesty."

Later, letters that foresee *"la mort Allemande."* In the last one, of March 1939: "I am out of the world. I can only suffer martyrdom."

After this, the chaos of the war years. When Italy enters the war, Edmond Jabès, an Italian citizen, is arrested by the British. He is set free a month later, when his father-in-law is able to show the antifascist pamphlets Edmond had published as early as 1929. In 1942, Egypt breaks off diplomatic relations with Vichy France, Rommel advances on El-Alamein, and Edmond is evacuated to Palestine with other militant antifascists by the British. Arlette works with the British Red Cross in hospitals, takes care of refugees.

When communication becomes possible again, Edmond tries to find Max Jacob through the Apostolic Delegation in Cairo. Answer: deceased. On March 5, 1944, in the concentration camp of Drancy.

•

The game of translation. The stakes of translation. The travail of translation. The hard work of travel through the boundless space of a book on the other side of the border. Go expecting trouble, go out prepared. "A strange voyage," Dominique Grandmont calls translating, "from which one may not return."

The "grid" of English over a text in French? Is it like superimposing a Mercator projection over a map as we know it? Or the other way round? The mismatch of the two grids is the challenge. As William Carlos Williams says in "Patterson":

A dissonance
in the valance of Uranium
led to the discovery

Dissonance
(if you are interested)
leads to discovery

Grid of language. *Sprachgitter.* Both weave and prisonhouse.

"Writing is an act of silence, allowing itself to be read in its entirety." For it, we must "rather than to sense, hold on to the silence that has formed the word."

And translating? Reading what is written *and* the silence behind it? Then writing what is written and what is hidden? I will come back to this.

•

"Silence is a form" (Claude Royet-Journoud).

•

In spring 1971, Paul Auster comes to Paris, just out of college. Claude Royet-Journoud introduces him to Jabès, with whom he very much wants to talk. Edmond proposes a free hour. Paul insists, could he not come a couple of hours earlier? He has so much to talk about. Edmond is intrigued. The next time we see him we ask:

"How was the afternoon with Paul?"

And Edmond, with what he has called his Oriental technique of answering a question:

"Let me tell you a story. There once was a sailor shipping out to South America. When he said goodbye to his best friend, he asked: is there anything you would like me to bring you back?

"The friend said: I have always wanted a parrot.

"The sailor promised to bring one.

"The sailor went to South America. He signed on for another voyage. A year or more went by. Finally he returned to Marseille and the moment he got off the boat realized he had forgotten all about his friend's parrot. He ran to the nearest pet shop, but the shop was out of parrots. The only big bird in the shop was an owl. What could he do? He bought the owl and took it to his friend: Here's your parrot. The friend was delighted.

"The sailor shipped out again. Another year went by. When he came back he went to see his friend. They talked, and after a while the sailor asked, a little sheepishly: How's the parrot?

"Oh fine, fine.

"Ah. . . . Does it. . . . . . . talk?

"Well, not yet. But I'm teaching it. And it is soooooo attentive.

"This is what Paul was like. He sat there and just looked at me with his big, beautiful eyes."

Arlette, who has not yet met Paul, but has heard of his looks, says: "I must meet *ce beau hibou*."

•

If I were writing a biography I would have to begin with Edmond Jabès's origins. But where are they? In Egypt, the desert, yes. The haute-bourgeoisie, the milieu of finance, a Jewish community that tries to balance French language and culture with Oriental surroundings? I am tempted to say, only the desert stayed with him, respecting no borders. But this is of course false.

One summer we take a charter back to the States that leaves from Brussels. We wonder how much money we'll need to change for the taxi from the station, etc. Edmond, without a moment's hesitation, without consulting the newspaper:

"The current rate is x Belgian Francs to y French Francs, you'll need about . . ."

My mouth drops open at this sudden surfacing of the stockbroker who *of course knows* such things.

It is from the world of the stockmarket that the desert saved him. He has called his trips into the desert

> a life-saving break *(une coupure salvatrice)*. It fulfilled an urgent need of both body and mind, and I would venture into it with completely contradictory desires: to lose myself so that, one day, I may find myself.

It was an experience of silence that

> makes you feel the nearness of death so deeply that it becomes difficult to bear any more of it. Only the nomads can withstand being squeezed in such a vise, because they were born in the desert.

•

For me, Edmond Jabès's origin is in the book. It is where I first encountered him. It is his deep connection with Judaism, with the people of the book: "[I]n traditional Judaism I have favored what comes through the book and what makes of the Jews the people of the book. There lies my true origin." It is his personal mythology: the author is created by the book while he creates it. His life span is that of the book. He is at best a catalyst who allows words to come together. At the end of the book, he is no longer needed and is rejected. "The writer is nobody." Echoes of Nietzsche? "There is no actor behind the act—the act is everything."

This is a stance that has become fashionable under the buzz word "death of the author." But with Edmond Jabès, it comes out of experience, is lived. It is no doubt a way of cauterizing his wound, the amputation from his native space. Rejected by the land of his birth he must create himself anew. So he defensively parries "no land" with "nobody." But, in compensation, a godlike nobody, a pure creator absorbed into his act of creation and visible only in it.

A creator who resolutely takes up residence in the word, solidly within the tradition of the Jews, the People of the Book, whose gift to civilization, in Blanchot's words,

> is not so much the revelation of the one God, but the revelation of the word as the place where men can be in relation to what excludes all relation: the infinitely Distant, the absolutely Foreign. God speaks and man speaks to him . . . the word spans the abyss.

Or, as Edmond Jabès puts it: "God will speak to us in the language we happen to speak." And as this language is French for Edmond Jabès, and is moreover the language he writes in, it is not surprising he settled in France rather than Israel.

But is the word, for all that, "the promised land where exile turns into home," as Blanchot would have it? Not quite. Not in our century. The word too bears the wound of the Holocaust: "We can no longer pronounce even everyday words the same way," Jabès says to Philippe de Saint-Chéron. And, as Lançon sees it, Jabès has merely traded the real desert for a more fleeting substitute and is "wandering in the desert of signs." But at least the latter is a desert that cannot "kick him out the door," a "non-place" from which one cannot, by definition, be expulsed.

> The experience of the desert is both the place of the Word—where it is supremely word—and the non-place where it loses itself in the infinite.

> A book is perhaps the loss of all place, the non-place of the place lost.
>
> A non-place like a non-beginning, non-present, non-knowing, an emptiness, a blank.

But I must qualify: it is the books of his maturity that Edmond Jabès feels created by, from *The Book of Questions* on, though he admits the poems collected in *Je bâtis ma demeure*. He rejects everything before 1943, which means seven books published over thirteen years, beginning in 1930. At the colloquium on his work at Cerisy-la-Salle, in August 1987, he regrets that nobody spoke of *Je bâtis ma demeure*, because writers tend to forget about their "eldest sons," and he quotes (with emotion, say the participants) "a first poem from this collection"—from 1942. He does not speak of his early books to me or any of his friends, as far as I know. He is, in fact, not entirely pleased when Keith finds a secondhand copy of *L'Obscurité potable,* a GLM chapbook of 1936.

"At least it's not *Maman!*"

Marcel Cohen every once in a while comes across a copy of Edmond's second book, *Je t'attends.* He always buys the copy to take it out of circulation because he knows Edmond would not like it to be taken as representing his work.

•

We are talking about Picasso. Françoise Gilot and Carleton Lake's *Life With Picasso* has just been published in France. Or perhaps it is when Edmond tells us how one of the few objects of value he was able to take with him in 1957 was a Picasso drawing. It allowed him to buy his apartment in Paris.

"Il était dur, Picasso."

"Did you ever meet him?"

"No. But he was hard. And not just with women. You know, Max Jacob had taken him in when he first came to Paris. Then, in 1944, when Jacob was arrested by the Nazis and taken to the concentration camp Drancy, friends asked Picasso to try and do something for him. All he said was: "Max is an angel. He won't need us to fly out of his prison."

•

Whenever I ask Edmond Jabès:

"Which of the two (or more) meanings of this word is more important?"

He answers: "Both."

Je suis le livre is both "I follow the book" and "I am the book."

He will not choose. Of course not. The Name of God holds all the words in the language. How could he give preference to one single meaning!

I have to choose. Limit. Narrow down. Cowardly, I put: "I follow the book." But it hurts to eliminate the other possibility.

When I read *Le Parcours,* a later book, I am even more sorry about my choice. Here it is unambiguous:

> What is a writer? What is a Jew?
> Neither Jew nor writer has any self-image to brandish. *"They are the book."*

And a few pages earlier: "I have been this word."

In the beginning was the word. In the beginning was man. Man of the word. Man of the book. Man of writing.

> A man of writing is a man of the four letters which form the unpronounceable Name. God is absent through His Name.
>
> Turning to the book must mean having guessed that we metamorphose in the word. . . .
>
> I took you in as a word.
> "I" is the book.

•

Man of the word. Man of the book. Man of writing. How I wish English had a good one-syllable word for "human being," like the German *Mensch*. But of course French also uses *l'homme* as the universal, and this is an asymmetry, a *donnée* of language, that Jabès never questions.

When Edmond is sent a questionnaire: "Is there an *écriture féminine?*" by a journal, he tells me he is going to answer something like:

"Writing is not the activity of a single person. I am only one partner in the process. It is an interaction between the writer and language. So the gender of the writer is of very limited importance, except in as far as it determines the experiences the writer draws on."

I agree on the crucial role of language—except, of course, that Edmond seems to assume that it is gender neutral. Which is hard to believe when *man* represents all of *man*kind!

I share his doubts about labeling certain ways of writing as "feminine," but rather because the application of archetypes is reductive. Every writer is androgyne. Imaginative writing is inclusive.

But at least while translating Edmond Jabès: if I accept "God" as a metaphor I may as well accept "man" as a metonymy.

•

The speed with which Keith and I become close to Edmond and Arlette is only paralleled in our friendship with Claude Royet-Journoud and Anne-Marie Albiach. *Coup de foudre*. I do not exaggerate when I inscribe my poem "Dark Octave" to Edmond: *avant de vous connaître je vous connaissais déjà.*

The times we spent together, the two almost-years, the summers, even the shorter visits in the U.S. have fused into a single time for me, a time outside time. Of joy and intensity. Of walking and talking. Of meals and laughter. Of jokes. Of concentrated work and vertiginous horizons. And a time of silences, the silence of a thought forming and the silence of being comfortable together.

A present. In both the obvious senses. Not continuous, alas. Oscillating, rather, the distance now zero, now immeasurable. Certainly a gift. And, in a third sense, the present of language, which is both the place and the time of our encounter. "Language," says Bernard Noël, "even though it is a great manipulator of time, leads everything back to the present."

•

After Edmond's death I haunt Arlette. After Arlette's death I haunt his streets as if I could read them. Rue de l'Epée de Bois, rue des Patriarches, rue Mouffetard, rue Ortolan, rue St. Médard, place de la Contrescarpe, rue Rollin with its lozenge stairway, rue Monge, rue Gracieuse, rue Pestalozzi. Rue de l'Arbalète, rue Daubenton, rue de Mirbel, rue Puits de l'Ermite, rue de la Clef.

The Paris streets in Jabès's work are not described the way a novelist might describe how the houses connect, how a woman stands at a window, safe behind the glass, and looks out at the wind whipping the sycamores, how the market invades the sidewalk on Saturday morning with its melons and figs next to the sturdier beans and potatoes, cheeses, patés. A market with gestures careful of eggs, of berries.

If there were to be such images they would have to be of Egypt. For that is, once and for all, his "image of a place," he tells film-maker Michelle Porte. But there is more to it. Gabriel Bounoure wrote as early as 1965:

> The Jewish poet today cannot stay within the kind of writing that used to reflect immediate life,—because this immediate life has been overtaken, stolen from him by those experiences called love, death, the horror of History, the great wave of the indeterminate.

So Jabès's streets appear as words. Magic names. They must speak so that we can see them. Even so, as he walks through them he walks through the desert, a chessboard, the night.

> A chessboard is the world of the city man. Have you noticed that every field, black or white, corresponds to an identical field in the sky? To go through a part of town means also going through a part of the night or the day. Here, you are at a certain crossing and at a certain imaginary intersection of the void.

"A thing does not exist," Edmond says often, "unless it has a name. But to name is already to interpret." And Jean Tortel takes this yet a step farther: "The eye sees nothing of the object but its name."

Even when he walks in the streets of Paris Edmond Jabès walks in the non-place that he has chosen:

> This absence of place, as it were, I claim as my own. It confirms that the book is my only habitat, the first and also the final. Place of a vaster non-place where I live.

This absence of place he also calls the place of love, invoking an openness beyond any narrow attachment:

> This place is love. It is absence of place.

•

I see Edmond at his desk, amid piles of paper. He puts down the book he had been holding. Moment of deliberation, suspended gravity, certain of one thing, the need to write. Out of the fog. Out of "Ed, or the first mist," that went up from the earth, "and watered the whole face of the ground," so God could create man "in the way a baker adds water and then kneads the bread."

I am suspicious of these passages, of my memory, of the stance of the observer. Not at ease with my eye. I say I see—and see only absence.

One of the meanings of Latin *lego,* "I read," is "I collect" or "gather"—a game of "Legos." I read my memories. I reread and recall. I collect and compose.

•

As I write this I learn of another friend's death. I see why it has taken me so long to be able to do this gathering. Here it is again, the falling away of the words. Again, I just want to roll my body in a tight ball.

The beginning, the exergue, of *Le Livre de l'Hospitalité*, the last book Edmond Jabès finished:

> To write, now, only to make known that one day I ceased to exist; that everything around me turned blue, an immense empty space for

the flight of an eagle whose powerful wings forever beat goodbye to the world.

Yes, only to confirm that I ceased to exist the day the rapacious bird by itself occupied the space of my life and the book, to rule as master and devour what, once more, was searching to be born of me, what I tried to express.

Useless the book where there is no hope for words.

As if he had known.

•

"Grief-muscles" (Darwin).

•

Translation as displacement. Literally from one language and culture to another. Literally also, within the text. Often I cannot duplicate, not even approximate, the assonances, rhymes, puns where they occur in the French text.

But I can place assonances, rhymes, wordplay elsewhere. So that the overall effect is similar. Though never the same.

This means the unit of translation has to be the whole work. Not the word as Walter Benjamin would have it, not the sentence or the line, though all of these have to be respected to the utmost.

"The whole surround," C. D. Wright said. We were talking about the unit of poetry, which for me has grown from single word to whole poem as I have become more interested in syntax, juxtaposition, what happens *between*.

C. D. concurred: "I used to think the line was the basic unit of the poem, and when I felt that I thought I knew what I was doing. Once that feeling started sliding away, my first reaction was paralysis. Then I got energized again even by the fear."

•

Statement and song. Their seemingly natural fusion in the original. Their overt tension in the process of translating. But does writing not always come out of tension, mismatch, disagreement?

As Giorgio Agamben says, with a narrower focus on enjambment:

> a mismatch, a disconnection between the metrical and syntactic elements, between sounding rhythm and meaning, such that (contrary to the received opinion that sees in poetry the locus of an accomplished and perfect fit between sound and meaning) poetry lives, instead, only in their inner disagreement.

•

"The whole surround" is more accurate than "the whole work." Translation must also understand what Hans-Georg Gadamer calls the "motivational space" of the work. This seems a matter of course for texts of earlier times. Pound introduced his translations of Cavalcanti by saying: "It is conceivable the poetry of a far-off time or place requires a translation not only of word and of spirit, but of 'accompaniment,' that is, that the modern audience must in some measure be made aware of the mental content of the older audience." But it holds also for contemporary works. We must understand what Walter Benjamin has described as the intentionality of a work, the ways in which it relates to its language and culture, to the "world of expression that precedes it, supports it and *both permits and impedes* what it wants to say," as Michèle Cohen-Halimi so cogently puts it. So that translating, like writing, must "stretch toward an *encompassing* grasp of each *single body*. How read *this* word without reading *the* word?"

Nobody will be surprised that I found it helpful to read in the Mishnah, the Pirke Aboth, when I began translating *The Book of Questions* with its texture of rabbinical commentary, its "generalized Talmudism," as François Laruelle calls it. Edmond Jabès's earlier poems come out of Surrealism, which which I was very familiar. But *The Book of Questions* fuses this with an altogether different tradition. I needed to get a sense of the form in which traditional rabbinical commentary has been received into English. Herbert Danby's translation did not give me the language I was looking for.

The diction is stiff and several notches too elevated. But it gave me a sense of the rhythm of question and answer, text and commentary, disparate voices in colloquy.

If I had known more at the time I would also have consulted Arabic works in the "divan" form, like *The Wedding Nights* of Abd al-Rahmane al-Souyoûti, which have a similar structure of guests assembling on various occasions to tell stories, argue, quote and discuss poems and philosophers.

Edmond Jabès actually read both Kabbalah and Arabic literature fairly late in his life. "Well after the first volumes of *The Book of Questions,*" he tells Jason Weiss. After people had remarked on his relation to these works, "as if wanting to check the intuition I had regarding a certain Judaism."

> It is clearly not the letter of those texts that marked me, but the shape of the thinking [*moule de pensée*], their spiritual depth, their so particular logic. . . .

In the early years of my knowing him Edmond seemed reluctant to acknowledge that these traditions stand behind his work. Speaking of rabbis he even put in a book: "But he owes them nothing." What gall! He owes them lots. But it is true that he does not owe them his work, this extraordinary fusion of traditions from East and West, that defies classification as well as direct literary filiation. To the point where, as Marcel Cohen has said, "they seem to try to go back to a space before literature, where the idea is still prisoner of its mother-lode (*gangue*)."

•

We work in my apartment, rue des Saints-Pères. The Jabèses' apartment is being painted. It is very quiet on this inner court. The *accumulateur* is no match for the damp cold. Edmond shivers.

"My body is still Egyptian."

Then goes on: "It's strange that we are sitting here together. We might easily never have met. I might have stayed in Cairo. You in

Germany and the U.S.: another world. Your path might never have crossed mine."

"I guess we met in *The Book of Questions*."

"We are still meeting in the book."

•

Back from a trip to Italy, Edmond tells with great amusement how he saw a car stopped at a red light, luggage rack piled high. In those few moments a couple of guys run up, untie the luggage, and make off with it. A policeman is standing by, watching the scene. The driver jumps out of the car and shouts at the policeman: Do something! Stop them! The policeman shakes his head: They are so poor, they need it so much more than you.

•

Keith and I are astonished that Edmond Jabès, born in Cairo, of French language and culture, used to have an Italian passport. This is how Keith remembers the story:

> It is from Edmond Jabès—*best story teller*—that we first heard how, in 1929, Egyptian citizenship was instituted. It was given to anyone with an Ottoman birth certificate or proof that his family had not held any foreign citizenship since 1848. The Jews, in Cairo immemorially, found this almost impossible because birth certificates issued by religious authorities were not accepted. Anyone not Egyptian by these new standards must have a passport from some other country. Of course, the Jews had none.
>
> Someone in the Italian embassy, remembering that the town hall of some city (Ferrara, was it?) had recently burned down—making verifications impossible—issued Italian passports to thousands of Jews. It was philantropic and—they were not issued gratis—profitable.
>
> When, many years later, at the Suez crisis, the Jews were more effectively expelled, a good number settled into their place of citizenship, Italy.

It is true that Edmond Jabès's grandfather had chosen Italian citizenship as early as 1882, at the time of Orabi Pascha's revolt. But there had not been any such thing as Egyptian nationality until 1929. From this point on, when he was seventeen, Edmond Jabès was officially a foreigner in his homeland. Doubly so since his Italian "nationality" corresponded neither to his language, French, nor to his country. Exile began even before he was physically exiled. Is it surprising that his work is an intense questioning of place?

•

Jabès's texts inhabit a space of "displacements and reductions," as Celan had said of Rilke's French, only much more so, with his physical existence at stake. His is the kind of text Celan speaks of in "The Meridian":

> The poem holds its ground, if you will permit me another extreme formulation, the poem holds its ground on its own margin. In order to endure, it constantly calls and pulls itself back from an "already-no-more" into a "still-here."
>
> This "still-here" can only mean speaking. Not language as such, but responding—not just verbally—"corresponding" to something. . . .
>
> This "still-here" of the poem can only be found in the work of poets who do not forget that they speak from an angle of reflection which is their own existence, their own physical nature.

How could such texts be "not just *übersetzt*, translated, but *über-gesetzt,* translocated"?

•

Again and again, Edmond Jabès repeats: The writer is nobody. The writer is a shadow. A writer knows only that he writes. A writer commits suicide at the threshold of the book. More than that: the writer is written.

"You are the one who writes and is written."

Our language—against the ground of silence behind it—defines us.

> Language is the—if not absolute, at least sensible—means by which man at the same time gives form to himself and to the world, or, rather, becomes conscious of himself by projecting a world outside himself. *(Wilhelm von Humboldt)*

More: language is our being. Agamben almost paraphrases Celan's "This 'still-here' can only mean speaking":

> That which is always already demonstrated in every act of speaking . . . (Aristotle, Aquinas), that which is always already indicated in speech without being named, is, for philosophy, being. The dimension of meaning of the word "being" . . . coincides with the taking place of language.

It is language that is. It is language that writes.

The writer may want to tell only the tragic love of Sarah and Yukel, "but the space around them is alive with the signs of their origin." There are words that cannot be kept from slipping in because words have a life of their own. The author writes and is written.

Not "inspiration." Not a variant of *"je est un autre,"* not another voice that speaks through him. Rather, there is a curious space where words exist before they come to live in the book. It is not the "code," not the system of the language as such. It is a step closer to utterance than to the system, a kind of limbo of utterance, which the writer explores.

> The pages of the book are doors. Words go through them, driven by their impatience to regroup, to reach the end of the work, to be again transparent. . . . Light is in their absence, which you read.

The writer's task is to lure the words onto the page. And they are willing and even eager to go there, but on their own terms.

They have their own order and fight their own battles. They use the page to make love and then leave again. The writer is the catalyst. The words use him/her to come into existence, but once the elements have come together he is eliminated.

"I am absent because I am the teller. Only the tale is real." "The writer is nobody." Yet he is the source of the tale.

"The artist belongs to the work, and not the work to the artist" (Novalis).

•

> A bad book is perhaps simply a book badly read by its author.

"The first sentence is free," Edmond Jabès says somewhere. "It could be anything. But already the second must follow from the first. And the third from the first two. You must read what you have written. If you read correctly what you have written, the text writes itself."

Here is another, narrower sense in which "we can only write what we have been given to read." We can only write what we have given ourselves to read.

•

All poetry is, in the end, translation, says Novalis. It translates "natural" language into the language of art *(Kunstsprache)*. In this process it elevates ordinary language to the state of mystery and leads it back home to the song that was its origin.

"The poet comes at language like a translator," echoes Valéry, and goes a notch higher in glorifying the result: "a peculiar kind of translator who translates ordinary discourse, modified by emotion, into the 'language of the gods.' "

For Edmond Jabès, too, the writer is a translator. "We write only what we have been allowed to read." And again:

> Writing a book means joining your voice with the virtual voice of the margins. It means listening to the letters swimming in the ink like

> twenty-six blind fish before they are born for our eyes. . . . Then I shall have said what I had to say and *what every page already knew.*

But he reverses the direction. Jabès starts out from the infinite, which is the ultimate goal of poetry in German Romantic theory.

He bypasses the issue of "ordinary" or "natural," language. Or, rather, he has altogether more respect for it than Novalis or Valéry. It is, after all, part of the Name of God. Its potential is, if not infinite, almost so; and the writer translates only part of it.

So, instead of elevating natural language into the "language of the gods," with Jabès, we translate the "language of the gods," the Name of God, the "book" of the infinite, into our more limited actual idiom. Writing/translating does not exalt, it narrows, as any passage from the potential to the actual must. It betrays experience with its contingencies—how much more does it betray sheer potentiality. In spite of its labyrinthine turns, its immense abundance of signs, our writing remains finite. The "book" of the infinite never surrenders. Worse, our narrowing of it is fatal, the finite by definition kills the infinite:

> The meandering word dies by the pen, the writer by the same weapon turned back against him.
>
> "What murder are you accused of?" Reb Achor asked Zillieh, the writer.
>
> "The murder of God," he replied. "I will, however, add in my defense that I die along with Him."

The writer/translator kills and is killed, writes and is written. The writer translates/kills God and at the same time identifies with Him in the role of creator who will be translated/killed by his creation. The word kills. "It cannot name something without removing that thing's presence," says Maurice Blanchot, following Hegel, "a sign that death speaks when I speak." And writing kills the word even while giving it life: Elya, the child of Yaël, of the word, is stillborn.

•

The relationship of author and word is tangled, a mutual dependence. But there are moments, the bleakest in all the books, when this relation breaks down and man is deprived of his essence:

> "Indeed. I once thought I would find my place in my words, but then. . . .
>
> "How shall I put it? The words suddenly proved to be different."
>
> "I'm not sure I understand." . . .
>
> "Well . . . as if, suddenly I could only speak through the silence of the spaces left empty by their difference."
>
> "Their difference?"
>
> "Some basic incompatibility between man and his words, something that keeps them apart . . ."
>
> "But isn't it always words which express us?"
>
> "No doubt, at the moment my pen draws them, when my voice sets them free. . . . But immediately after, I realize that I have not written, not spoken."
>
> "But in that case, what you read, what other people hear, what is that?"
>
> "A mixture of sounds, of words bitterly remote in their alien truth. Man is mute. I tell you. The only mute creature."

Better to be tormented by the words, to let the sentences be tattoos, arrows, insect-bites on his page of flesh. The writer is the book. The book is the writer's wound. The cause and the process are one. The process and the goal are one. Yet they are not:

> For I am writing
> and you are the wound.
> Have I betrayed you, Yukel?
> I have certainly betrayed you.

•

And the translator? Edmond Jabès knows: "We grow old through the word. We die of translation." And, with a chuckle, underlines the sentence in my copy.

I have certainly betrayed him. And taken pleasure in it.

Readers who read Edmond Jabès in English do not read Edmond Jabès. They do not read Rosmarie Waldrop either, but our dialogue and collaboration. A necessarily imperfect approximation trying to locate itself on that fine line that is as close as possible to the French yet as remote from it as necessary for the text to stand on its English feet, as it were. In the space between. "Not resemblance," says Maurice Blanchot perhaps too optimistically, "but identity on the basis of otherness."

Güneli Gün: "Translating Pamuk is like mirroring his gestures." I like this analogy. But I am translating a work in which "a double mirror separates us from the Lord so that God sees Himself when trying to see us, and we, when trying to see Him, see only our own face." Which *n*th reflection does translation catch? Or am I setting up my own double mirror? Am I reading Edmond Jabès in such a way that my translation can resemble him?

I am again betraying Edmond Jabès in these pages. I put words in his mouth as if my memory were not notoriously poor. *English* words yet, which he never said. Words that cannot catch his tone, his *Ce n'est pas ça*. Sentences too complete, without interruption, assent or opposition, without the gestures that replace the "big" words or put them in quotation marks, without the smile that nuances a judgment, without the laugh, without the digressions and non sequiturs of conversation. Without body.

With quotations from his books to protect my rear, I speak for him. I choose and cadence.

•

From the beginning, one of the difficulties in translating Edmond Jabès is the distinction between *mot* and *parole*, a distinction that English covers over with one single term: "word." It is true we have "utterance," which has the oral dimension of *parole* and, if more weakly, the sense of its opposition to—and circular interdependence with—*langue*, the code of language. I try to use it, but often find it clumsy in its sentence. Except in cases where orality is crucial, I let the rhythm of the sentence determine the choice—most often in favor of "word." Not only is it one syllable and a fuller sound than "utterance," it is also weightier and more appropriate in its connotations. "Word" rather than "utterance" implies creation for us: "In the beginning was the word."

Vocable, occasional in the earlier books, then increasingly frequent, further complicates the situation. This lexical term evokes for Jabès "voice" and *vocare,* "to call," the word as sound—but an ugly sound in English. Sometimes I can go to "vocabulary" in spite of the fact that this meaning is secondary for Jabès. In his later years, in any case, this word becomes charged for him with a special, private meaning: he thinks of *vocable* as the spoken (and heard) word in the book, the oral dimension preserved within the written. "This word of silence," he says at the colloquium of Cerisy-la-Salle:

> What is important in the experience of the desert is the experience of the voice and also the experience of listening. In the desert, you hear before you see, and the nomads can tell what will appear only much later. I am sensitive to this phenomenon of listening and the voice. To such a point that I wanted to distinguish the utterance (*parole*) of the book from other utterances. The utterance of the book, *this word of silence,* I have called vocable.

•

Edmond speaks of the desert. He sometimes speaks of the Nile, its painted barges, the sound of the oud. Sometimes of Cairo, the old city, the bazaars, the cries of the merchants. He speaks of palms, baobabs, date and fig trees.

There are many things Edmond does not speak of, but Arlette does. Their life in Egypt. Their haute-bourgeoisie background. He waves it away with: "that has no importance." Though he is proud that his great-grandfather took care of the synagogue David Ibn Abi Zimra and built housing for the poor around it; that he himself was part of a literary circle that organized lectures, brought to Cairo Cavafy, Valéry, Cocteau–and boycotted Marinetti, by whose fascism Edmond, technically an Italian citizen, felt very deeply concerned.

Arlette tells how she saw miles of parquet stretching before her whenever she went toward her mother. How Edmond's mother remembered him coming home from kindergarten: "I've met a very nice little girl. Her name is Arlette." Though she herself remembers her *coup de foudre* on meeting him on a boat when she was fifteen and, according to family history, felt an instant, urgent need for high heels. She tells of their courtship. Of drives in Edmond's car where she rides slunk down in her seat for fear of being seen. She shows me their wedding picture and the photo where *Edie geule à la bourse*—where Edmond shouts his bids at the Cairo stock market, proving to his father-in-law that he can do more than write poems. His "Rudolf Valentino" look, another photo.

She tells stories of the health center she established for indigent Jews.

One day, an American film company needed extras for a biblical spectacular. Arlette sent her clients. Later some manager complained to her: they all walked off with their costumes!

In Paris, her experience at this center helped her get her job: supervising the health of researchers in nuclear physics.

Sometimes, when we are traveling together, she takes mischievous pleasure in telling me of Edmond's macho moments. For instance when, on some charity occasion not long after their marriage, she was supposed to be part of a chorus in grass skirts: "If you wear this I will go up on stage and slap you in front of everybody." Edmond scowls, looks out the window. A little revenge for her life of devotion?

About a year after Edmond's death, Arlette comes to visit us in London. I am surprised to hear she is studying Arabic.

"But you know Arabic."

"I know street Arabic. I want to be able to read.

"But," she goes on, "there is really nothing I want to do except talk about Edmond."

At his death, she says, she felt mostly anger. That he had left her. It has taken her almost a year to get over this feeling, to be able to mourn him.

If her count is right this leaves her seven months of mourning before she follows him.

•

What neither Edmond nor Arlette talk much about: how the situation of Egyptian Jews became more and more difficult after 1945, with Arab nationalism growing dominant. I read about it now, in Daniel Lançon's *Jabès l'Egyptien*. The League of Arab States was founded in Cairo in March 1945, clearest sign of the new strength of the pan-Arab movement. Anglo-Egyptian negotiations broke down in 1945 and again in 1946, which led to antiforeign and anti-Jewish riots, complete with burning of a synagogue. The government blew hot and cold, now declaring that Jews are an integral part of Egyptian society, now ordering them to take part in a census of foreigners (1947). When the State of Israel was founded in 1948, this was considered an act hostile to the entire Middle East, and Jews in general came to be regarded as the public enemy. Jews were put under house arrest except for special permits (May 1948), certain professions closed to foreigners (September 1948), including that of stockbroker, which Edmond nevertheless continued to exercise until 1956. From October 1949 on, Egypt was free to expulse all foreigners without notice. From 1952 on, foreigners were obliged to obtain a *carte de résidence*. On June 19, 1953, a year after General Mohamed Naguib's coup, the republic was proclaimed with Naguib as president and Gamal Abdel Nasser as vice president—and, at first, welcomed by Edmond Jabès as a necessary alternative to being a British colony and as a promise of social reforms. In 1956, with the Algerian war, the nationalization of the Suez Canal, and the ensuing French/English attack on Egypt, the crisis became acute. "Foreign" property was confiscated, bank accounts frozen, Edmond Jabès's included. Harrassed and threatened with imprisonment, Edmond and Arlette left in June 1957.

Strangely enough, in Cairo I felt closer to—I could say more dependent on—French culture than in Paris. I should add that my uprooting was total and happened practically from one day to the next. . . . In Paris, the earth opened under my feet.

•

Keith remembers our meeting Arlette's mother:

> Madame Cohen, Arlette's mother, was in her eighties. Small, frail, looking bleached, a little deaf. She read voraciously, in several languages. Claude found her sexy.
>
> It was hard for Edmond to work with her in the apartment. Just when he got into a train of thought, she would break in with something like, "Edie, what do you think of Shakespeare?"
>
> We were introduced to her as writers. She tells us, in perfect English, that she has been reading a book she does not *entirely* understand. Perhaps we could help her.
>
> Certainly we will try. What is the book?
>
> *Finnegans Wake.*

•

Obsession with the Book, the written word. But also with the spoken word, with dialogue, even if it is impossible, lost between pre-dialogue and post-dialogue, between preparatory silence and after-silence.

> . . . the actual dialogue, vital, irreplaceable, but which, alas, does not take place: it begins the very moment we take leave of one another and return to our solitudes.

Dialogue, like the present moment, impossible to hold in its passage from future to past. We are left with pre- or post-. It is another empty center, absent like the story, the text. Like God. Potential to be or not. Long years of after-silence.

Ortega y Gasset has a similar intuition of how dialogue "gives birth to silence":

> When we converse, we live within a society; when we think, we remain alone. But in this kind [of true interchange], we do both at once . . . : we pay attention to what is being said with almost melodramatic emotion and at the same time we become more and more immersed in the solitary well of our meditation. This increasing dissociation cannot be sustained in a permanent balance. For this reason, such conversations characteristically reach a point when they suffer a paralysis and lapse into a heavy silence. Each speaker is self-absorbed. Simply as a result of thinking, he isn't able to talk. Dialogue has given birth to silence, and the intitial social contact has fallen into states of solitude.

If we now look back on the final non-dialogue between Edmond Jabès and Paul Celan, Ortega allows us to see it in a gentler light than Edmond Jabès did, almost as unavoidable, as an illustration, or extreme point, of the nature of interchange:

> Exchange of words, closeness. His voice? Soft, most of the time. And yet it is not his voice I hear today, but his silence. It is not him I see, but emptiness, perhaps because, on that day, each of us had unawares and cruelly revolved around himself.

•

Paul Celan said to Jean Daive:

> Insanity—the only insanity [*démence*]—does not lead to being obsessed with death. It leads to rejection of dialogue. To take on the lightning from the sky. Yes. I am speaking to you, no? To take on fear [*la frayeur*]. Yes. Who is afraid? But to take on the body of the incommunicable. No. Dialogue, the obsession with dialogue, the imminence of dialogue: a madness [*folie*].

Dialogue, our impossible salvation. And our madness.

•

The "Hand of Fatima" on Edmond's desk. Hand next to hand. Ornate silver hand next to live hand. Lucky hand and writing hand.

All the letters I have from him are handwritten. I complain:
"They are hard to decipher."
"So much the better. You'll spend more time thinking about me!"
He seems to think it a bit impolite that I type mine.

All his manuscripts are handwritten, are literally manuscripts. Arlette types them.

•

But what is the "law of their own" that words follow? It is not their history. Jabès does not (or only rarely) pursue etymology. He does not so much dig down in time as unfold. He does not so much probe accretions of past usage as a horizontal, synchronic dimension: the law of the words' material being, their body of sound and letters. And the way that Edmond Jabès listens to these affinities—these rhymes, assonances, alliterations, homophones, puns, permutations of letters, words buried within words—is, for all his anxiety, so joyous, so *amorous* that the pleasure is truly contagious.

"One letter in common is enough for two words to know each other." In his own initials, Edmond Jabès discovers *je* (I) as well as *jeu* (game), and fire (*feu*) in leaf or page (*feuille*) along with eye (*oeil*). We are alone (*seul*) at the threshold (*seuil*). The written (*écrit*) and the tale (*récit*) are "one and the same word with its letters scrambled in a most natural way. All writing offers its share of the telling." Even though being (*l'être*) is a letter (*lettre*), the book (*livre*), as we know, never surrenders (*se livre*).

The similarity of sound governs the course of the sentence, the direction of thought. *Dialogue* brings with it the *diamond* that sparkles in the *facets* of conversation. Some know only the worm (*ver*) in truth (*vérité*) and ignore its nature, which is vertigo (*vertige*).

The spelling *feu-oeil* for *feuille* makes me wonder whether "*feu-oeil* meant for him 'dead eye' or, on the contrary, 'eye of fire.' The latter fits rather better with my idea of the white page in whose eye the word is consumed."

A whole chapter in *The Book of Yukel*, "Portrait of Sarah and

Yukel in Seed and Sign," grows out of the fact that the word *or* (gold) glitters in the words *mort* (death) and *sort* (fate).

I can only conclude with Wilhelm von Humboldt that "the force of thinking gathers in a word like light clouds in a serene sky."

It is language that writes. It is language that thinks.

> Reading Kabbalistic texts shows us the Name in motion as if it refused to stay itself. . . . The tradition of Midrash teaches that there are 70 faces for each word, even for each letter. When a new Name or word appears it is a new face surfacing, not a deformation.
>
> *(Marc-Alain Ouaknin)*

•

Edmond Jabès is careful to distance himself from his early Surrealism. "The Surrealist image seduced us, struck us, but was autonomous, like something added on," he tells Serge Fauchereau. He is equally not part of Concrete Poetry even though some of his procedures and statements ("I look at the words, which are already a kind of image") seem to suggest a closeness. His aim is not to invert the traditional hierarchy of sense over sound, but to establish parity between them or, rather, to establish a dynamic relation between language and thinking, where the words do not express preexisting thoughts, but where their physical characteristics are allowed to lead to new thoughts. Once the physical properties and similarities of words have given the impetus, the semantic dimension is allowed full play to probe and develop the implications. Once "dialogue" has led to "diamond," we will hear about the nature of the diamond until its multiple facets lead us back to dialogue—now on the semantic level, to the multiple perspectives it allows to emerge. Or, as he puts it:

> Being an integral part of the text, the image for me no longer functions as an image. Anchored in thought, in the development, it is a shortcut in discourse, as if it were not there for its own sake, but for the sake of precision.

•

Especially in *El, or the Last Book*, Edmond Jabès constantly breaks open words for other words contained inside them. He reads them to pieces, he *lit aux éclats*, in good Kabbalistic fashion. Or, in Felix Philipp Ingold's words, he finds the polysemic in the homophonic.

Once more, commentary:

> "In the word *commentaire*," he repeated, "there are the words *taire, se taire, faire taire*, 'to be silent, to fall silent, to silence,' which quotation demands."

Much as Edmond Jabès wants me to parallel his procedures he does not want the translation to play with any of the English words contained in "commentary": come, Mary, coat, core, corn, comet, money, macro, tar, tarry, etc. When he writes: *L'arbre est dans le marbre*, "The tree is in the marble," he rejects the possibilities of "mar," "bar," "lamb," or even "real," words that are *in* our English "marble" in the way *arbre* is contained in *marbre*. Small wonder. For him, word-play means the words are playing with us. It shows language thinking, unfolding associations, and creating new, unorthodox meanings. Not just word-play, but word-work. His figures of speech are always also figures of thought. He does not want his thought deflected from the direction *his* language pointed to.

There is nothing for it but to leave the French word and explain. Awkward. But it also lets difference, foreignness come to the fore. Makes us aware of the space *between* the languages where translation lives.

Still, I am happy when I can save the music without going too far astray. "Croire pour croître" stands by itself as an aphorism. The organic implication of "growing" is not developed in what follows, so a different kind of enlargement, of outreach, becomes possible: "To have faith in order to fathom."

I cannot duplicate the pun in "Sans racines. Cent racines." I can at least have a rhyme: "No roots. Grow roots." But on the same page, I am helpless before the play on *écrit* and *récit* already mentioned.

> . . . *écrit, récit,* the "written" and the "tale": one and the same word with its letters scrambled in a most natural way.
>
> "All writing offers its share of the telling," she said.

•

I talk to Edmond about the homophonic Catullus translations of Celia and Louis Zukofsky. I explain their desire to keep the sound of the words, almost phoneme by phoneme, while also conveying the meaning. Their translation, says the preface, "follows the sound, rhythm, and syntax of his Latin—tries, as is said, to breathe the 'literal' meaning with him." Edmond is impressed, as I am, by this focus on sound, by the impossible ambition to transfer *everything intact,* and by the Zukofskys' sheer persistence: they do not just tackle one poem or two in this manner, but *all* of Catullus. Edmond's English is not really good enough to realize quite how strange the Zukofskys' texts are, though he appreciates the brilliant successes like "Miss her, Catullus" for the famous opening, "Miser Catulle." Here, both the single sound and the whole poem enter into the translation because "missing her" is indeed at the root of Catullus's misery. But Edmond is immediately worried: why do I bring this up? Am I tempted to try something like it? He quickly draws the line: although he too wants *everything* transferred, when choice is inevitable, the line of thought, the way he develops the implication of words is more important to him than their sound.

I myself am fascinated by this project of "breathing the 'literal' meaning." When I look at Catullus 85 and find:

> O th'hate I move love. Quarry it fact I am, for that's so re queries.
> Nescience, say th'fiery scent I owe whets crookeder.

for:

> Odi et amo, quare id faciam, fortasse, requiris.
> nescio, sed fieri sentio et excrucior.

I am amazed that the English does indeed sound like the Latin, amazed by the sheer strangeness of diction which nevertheless manages to suggest some of the Latin's meaning. I am intrigued by the English words the Zukofskys heard in the Latin, by the meanings and associations the unexpected ones set in motion: quarry, fiery, owe, crookeder. I am in awe of this work, delighted that it exists. But I am also glad it is not the *only* Catullus in English. In fact, I tend to think of it more as Zukofsky than as Catullus. I think of the method ("his monstrous method," says Davenport) less as a window onto a foreign text than as a way of extending the possibilities of poetic speech in English and especially drawing attention to the material, physical nature of words. In other words, an extreme example of "foreignizing" curves back into an emphasis on the target language, in terms of a subversive poetics. Though it is the presentation *as* translation that makes the point.

•

Edmond Jabès's books are poetry. Not because they occasionally break into verse, but because their prose relies as much on rhythm and sound as on meaning.

> "How can I know if I write verse or prose," Reb Elati remarked. "I am rhythm."

Three rhythms layer the work. On the micro-level, there is the rhythm of the individual line or sentence. A rhythm that, in the verse, comes out of the tension between sentence and line, and in the prose, out of the tension between speech and the more formal syntax of writing. In either case, it is the tension of Zukofsky's "Lower limit speech/Upper limit music."

On the structural level, there is the rhythm of prose and verse and, more importantly, of question and answer, question and further question, question and commentary, commentary on commentary and, later, aphorism after aphorism.

Rhythm of Midrash, of the rabbinical tradition. Not a dialectic aiming for synthesis, but an open-ended spiraling. A large rhythm, come out of the desert, a rhythm of sand shifting as if with time itself.

Then, there is a third rhythm. It is on the level of the book: a rhythm of text and blank space, of presence and absence.

The white space at the end of a line of verse has been displaced: into the white spaces between paragraphs, between aphorisms. Not verse, it is still an art of turning. Toward the white of the page. Toward the silence, the continuity that carries the music. Toward what is not.

Bernard Noël pinpoints this rhythmic function of white space in an essay on Claude Royet-Journoud:

> Interruption always makes a double move as it places [the interrupted text] in a succession which in its entirety forms the poem. In other words, even if the verbal part of the poem is composed of a discontinuous sequence, it nevertheless develops in a continuous space. It is the role of the white space to suggest this continuity in spite of the pagination demanded by the form of the book.

I always have to fight for Jabès's blank spaces with the American publishers. The spaces always get whittled down, end up less generous than in the French editions. University of Chicago Press wants to eliminate them altogether.

"They don't change the meaning."

"They change the rhythm," I counter. "And that does change the meaning."

•

Perhaps there is a fourth rhythm, on the level of thought. The rhythm in which the book oscillates between the two frontiers of language:

Lower limit scream. / Upper limit silence.

•

When I meet Edmond Jabès, in 1971, I have already begun to write sequences rather than single poems. But it is Jabès's work that pushes me into thinking in terms of *books* (though there is also the example of Spicer). It is specifically Jabès's insistence on the book on the one hand (as the writer's only place, as Mallarmé's "spiritual instrument") and fragmentation on the other, that focuses my own contradictory impulses toward flow and fragment.

•

Edmond Jabès walks slowly. Long slow sentences. Not chewing on a single word, but always pushing on, step after step.

He loves the anecdote of Joyce telling a friend:

"I've spent all day on one sentence."

"I understand, *le mot juste* . . ."

"No. I have all the words."

•

Arlette's warmth ("No more hotels for you. You are going to stay with us")—and wit. Claude's navy sweater is worn through at the elbow. She knits him a big red patch, a *secours rouge* of his own. Later, when a friend's lover is hesitant to tell Edmond and Arlette that her child is by another man, Arlette immediately sends a baby toy: *"nous sommes vieux, mais pas vieux jeu."*

•

Edmond gets Keith and me invited to a party. "We will dance," he says.

I haven't danced in years and am a bit nervous. Edmond and Arlette are passionate and accomplished ballroom dancers. Once, on vacation, they stumble onto a tournament and join in. They are by far the oldest couple—and win first place with a tango. The young woman of the second couple is near tears until Edmond hands her the prize TV.

I did not see Edmond dance. But I see him do sketches where he plays all the parts with the help of a hat and a kerchief. I hear him recite a hilarious *La cigale et la fourmi* in a North African patois full of couscous and *kifkif*. I remember the two morals (or, rather, "mortals!") the ant pronounces at the end:

mortalité un:
tu bouffes tu crèves
tu bouffes pas tu crèves
alors tu choises
mortalité deux:
la loi du plus fort
a toujours raisoun
et le couscous arabe est superior

This is at Mitsou Ronat's, who seems depressed and needs cheering up. It is Joseph Guglielmi who dances on this occasion. A fabulous tango. With his wife Therese who later kills herself.

I see Edmond dance in his syntax, at certain matings of words, certain repetitions. Leaps and rounds.

•

It takes me one year to translate the first volume of *The Book of Questions*. It takes me four years to find a publisher. In 1976, Wesleyan University Press launches the book. I try to arrange a small reading tour to help promote it.

I come to know Edmond's anxiety of missing trains or boats. He obsessively rehearses the time table with me: When is our train? How do we get to the station? When will you call the taxi? Have you packed your bag? How do we get to the university?—until I cannot take it any more:

"I promise I will get you there, on time, but I don't want to talk about it."

Arlette chuckles. In Egypt, Edmond once claimed their boat departed a whole day earlier than it did and had the family spend the day in a hotel next to the harbor.

Then Edmond, who loves telling stories even when the joke is on him, tells how Arlette and he had reserved seats from Rome to Naples. They arrive very early and are astonished that the train is already rather full. In fact, their seats are taken. The couple seated there have reservations also. Angrily, the Jabèses find other seats and wait for the *controlleur*. Meanwhile, the train stops at a small town. And another. Finally the *controlleur* comes. He carefully looks at their tickets.

"Signore, may I ask you a personal question?"

Edmond almost explodes. First they issue double reservations, then the *controlleur* wants to ask him a "personal question"!

The question is:

"Signore, are you crazy? You have first-class reserved seats for the express and you travel third class in the local."

•

It is Marcel Cohen who reminds me of this story. I remember him almost silent in Edmond's company, listening. Now Marcel's stories fill not only the page, but the room. Though they, too, always leave a margin.

•

We serve Edmond and Arlette some pita bread. Delighted, Arlette exclaims: *C'est arabe*.

As she does when I put turmeric in a dish. As she does almost always when she likes something, or so I tease her. Do we carry the land of our birth with us? In our tastebuds?

And though "setting out to conquer the unknown shows perhaps only our secret hope to discover its resemblance to the known," she never says, it's *like* Arab bread. She installs, for a moment, her very youth in this piece of bread, this whiff of turmeric, of cumin, skipping the whole problem of resemblance that torments and excites Edmond—to the point where he projects it onto his God:

"In the beginning was the word that wanted to resemble."

The question of resemblance goes to the roots of thought and language, of all that proceeds by analogy, contrast, imitation. Was not man created in God's image? But in a universe where God not only has no image, but does not exist? Where He is an image made in the likeness of man? Then there is no basis on which we can build our systems. *The Book of Resemblances* explores our precarious constructions on this unreliable basis of resemblance, on this absence of firm foundation.

> "Can we be like Him, Who, in His essence, is without likeness?" asked Reb Eliav.
>
> He was told: "Are we not the image of the void which has no image?"

If we are the image of no image, it is small wonder the body is elusive and joins the ineffable:

> In front of the mirror, Sarah looks at her naked body. If she takes her time to examine it closely, it is because she knows it escapes her. . . .
>
> The mind reinvents the body. The body we see is in the image of thought, a—changing—image we maintain.
>
> Your body is a book of thoughts that cannot be read in its entirety.

•

Our very first readings in New York City are not auspicious. At New York University's *Maison Française,* all but three persons in the hall are friends I have alerted. A few minutes before the beginning, the director comes up to me:

"I know nothing about Jabès. I trust you can do your own introductions."

Edmond reads beautifully. With great simplicity. With a voice that is not quite his everyday talking voice, but not theatrical, not exaggerated either. It reins in the emotion, yet lets us know it is there. Resonant. Deep.

I count on the reading at the Graduate Center to make up for this less than perfect welcome. We are invited there by Alan Mandelbaum, who has met the Jabèses in 1971 through his nephew, Paul Auster, and has been their dinner guest.

The reading is in late afternoon. We arrive at the Graduate Center on Edmond time, early. It is a good thing, the corridors seem endless. A labyrinth of tunnels without thread, without necessity. We almost get lost, but still arrive at Alan Mandelbaum's office a good half hour in advance. He has us sit down and begins—or continues—to run in and out of the office in a frenzy of activity, now getting papers from the secretary, now calling me into a different room to talk about publication possibilities.

Edmond is a little puzzled, but excited by the idea of the Graduate Center, of an introduction by Henri Peyre whom he heard lecture in Cairo in 1934—and the full auditorium. Then Henri Peyre begins:

"Edmond Jabès is from Egypt. In Egypt everybody is a poet. I know this from personal experience . . ."

He proceeds to tell how, when he visited Egypt, the customs officer, seeing the poetry books in his suitcase, began to recite a poem in Arabic. On his return, the same officer passed him through without opening any bags, but not without handing him a small volume of his own poems. When Peyre finally has to say something about Edmond Jabès, he whips out a piece of paper and misreads most of the book titles.

I don't have to look at Arlette to know she is furious. But Edmond does not lose his cool. He thanks Professor Peyre with just the slightest touch of irony:

"I hope I will come up to your expectation."

After the reading, while students enthusiastically crowd around

Edmond, Alan Mandelbaum, who has excused himself with opera tickets, asks various staff members if they can have dinner with us in the Graduate Center restaurant. Most have other engagements by this time. I hear Mary Ann Caws come to the rescue: "Yes, I can. But I have to make a call first."

Unfortunately, Arlette hears it also and is aware of the makeshift nature of the arrangements. Nevertheless, a pleasant group assembles, and the dinner marks the beginning of Mary Ann Caws's friendship with the Jabèses.

•

Luckily Edward Kaplan, at Brandeis, and Richard Stamelman, at Wesleyan, couldn't be more enthusiastic in their welcome. And at Brown, I am on home turf.

At the party after the reading, though, Edmond is devastated. He talks with a pretty undergraduate. She compliments his English. He tells her that he was with the British army during the war.

"Was that the First World War?" she asks.

When I tell this to Marcel Cohen, he comments:

"This is Edmond's come-uppance. Once, when Arlette mentioned her mother's birthdate, Edmond asked: 'A.D. or B.C.?' "

•

Back in Paris, Edmond tells Michel Leiris of his reading tour in the U.S.

"And what do you do at these readings?"

"I read. My translator reads in English. And I talk about my books."

"Ah, you talk about your books. Do you talk well about your books?"

Edmond, a bit taken aback by the question: "I try to."

"I always found that writers who talk well about their books don't write very well."

Edmond tells me this with a big laugh: "He roundly made fun of me!"

•

But what is this *book* that never surrenders to us?

> Our text of origin: *the text which engenders all texts to be written and which, though ever elusive, will not leave off haunting us.*

I say "this" precisely because I cannot define it. I want to call it potentiality. But whatever name we give it—potentiality, God, the infinite, nothingness—it is the missing core, the empty transcendence, the unreachable center that Jabès's wandering questions circle.

This essential text, the originating silence of the possible, forever eludes our grasp. The divine Name is unpronounceable *because* it is the juxtaposition of *all* the words in the language and hence cannot be contained in any *one*. This potentiality, this fluid, dynamic plenitude is mirrored—on a small scale—in a text that refuses a single line of discourse, explodes it into fragments and facets, opens it to multiple perspectives, difference, ambiguity, multivalence—and, always, to the nothing, the absence underneath it all. Small wonder that these books are so impossible to summarize or to pin down to an argument.

•

> Man does not exist. God does not exist. The world alone exists through God and man in the open book.

At the end of his important essay, "Edmond Jabès et la question du livre," Jacques Derrida finds that, under all the questions of *Le Livre des Questions,* there is one non-question:

> The non-question I am talking about is the unshaken certainty that being is a Grammar; and the world through and through a cryptogram to constitute or reconstitute by poetic inscription or deciphering; that the book is the origin [*originaire*]; that everything is *in the book* before being *in the world* and in order to come there; that everything can be born only by *approaching* the book, can die only

> by failing *in regard to* the book; and that the impassive shore of the book is always *first*.

So that there is no "radical illegibility."

This essay is published in 1964 when only the first *Livre des Questions* has appeared. It is no doubt this essay that sharpens Jabès's eye to the implications of his work. For while the mirror structures of question and commentary as well as their ground of silence are present from the beginning, it is only in the later volumes that we find explicit statements about exactly this ultimate limit of language: a "radical illegibility" of the world. In *Yaël* (1967), for example: "Our lot is to interpret an undecipherable world." And along with this, increased probing of what escapes language: silence and body. ("Your body is a book of thoughts that cannot be read in its entirety.")

It shows how enclosed we are in the mirrors of our sign systems that both Derrida and Jabès can posit the radically unavailable only in semiotic terms, though of course negated: un-readable, undecipherable. It is because Jabès's thinking is bold enough to come to this absolute borderline where our signs are impotent, where we can at best *point* or *scream*, that his writing naturally turns "back on itself."

For Aristotle, it it only by thinking itself that thought can escape being caught between potential and act. Agamben comments:

> The aporia is here that supreme thought can neither think nothing nor think something, can neither stay potential nor pass into action, can neither write nor not write. It is to escape this aporia that Aristotle pronounces his famous thesis that thought thinks itself, a kind of median point between thinking nothing and thinking something, between potential and act. The thought that thinks itself does not think an object, nor thinks nothing: it thinks its pure potential (to think and not to think).

It is by turning back to examine its own process that the thought and writing of *The Book of Questions* concludes that "being is a grammar" *in as far as* it is accessible to us. For us (Agamben again) "the meaning of the word 'being' . . . coincides with the taking place of language," with utterance, with the act of speaking. We cannot get outside language. So perhaps the question is whether "being is a grammar" or "being is utterance." But since code and utterance, *langue* and *parole,* are interdependent, this question is perhaps idle.

There would be another way to go, which Jabès does not take: to question the nature of language itself, the way it is constructed by the social—for instance, the way it encodes universality as masculine. Jabès questions the ways of his thinking, but not its tool and matrix. Having made language his house and country, he has to hold on to it as his one secure anchor: "the only home of the Jewish people is the word," he tells Madeleine Chapsal. Though the "word" here is *parole*, utterance, which leaves the door open to change.

Yet there are moments when he feels that this anchor is not solid either: "In the middle of words is the void through which they escape." "In vain [the poet] has tried to retain being," Bounoure comments. "The letter is dead, probably of the same death as God," and as a consequence, "an irremediable 'ontic poverty' strikes all our works." It strikes even "the book where everything seems possible through a language that one thinks one can master and that finally turns out to be but the very *place* of its bankruptcy."

But this "ontic poverty" is in the very nature of language. It is precisely what makes it a medium for thought, what makes it able to adumbrate (if not capture) transcendence, even the empty transcendence of nothingness. Rather than cause for lament, these moments where the void invades and erodes the word are epiphanies (uncomfortable, it is true) of language, of its essential tie to death, annihilation, nothingness.

•

Negative Capability, that is when man is capable of being in uncertainties, Mysteries, doubts, without any irritable reaching after fact and reason. *(John Keats)*

"Jabès's books are not obscure," says Richard Stamelman. "They only become unreadable when one is looking for certainty. Their readability is dependent on the deferral of meaning."

•

Edmond often speaks, and with utmost reverence, of Maurice Blanchot—whom he has not met though they have exchanged letters and books for fifteen years. Blanchot does not see anybody. He claims to be living his "posthumous life." Edmond is proud of Blanchot's inscriptions in the books he sends, his *belles dédicaces*. And his letters which, he says, do not interrupt the silence. He feels the way Blanchot undermines narrative, dissolves it into speech, is close to his own project: "Your stories leave the grooves of storytelling and become sheer discovery of speech at its end, in its last inscribed, audible moments," he says in his essay, "The Unconditional."

Roger Laporte remembers this from the sixties, when Bergman's *Silence* was released in France:

> My wife and I went to the movie in rue de la Harpe. Blanchot arrived for the same showing. We go up to him to say hello, but he withdraws, mumbling something inaudible. We don't insist. We go back home (we live in Beauvais at that time). Two days later, we receive a letter in which Blanchot wrote more or less: "How marvelous to see you."

Edmond speaks of Michel Leiris, whom he sees once a week for lunch. He speaks of Paul Celan, René Char, Max Jacob. He shows me books by Gerard Macé, Jean-Claude Lebensztejn, Roger Lewinter, Ginevra Bompiani, Giorgio Agamben. He speaks of Jacques Derrida, Emmanuel Lévinas, Roger Caillois, Jean Starobinski, often of Gershom Scholem, Franz Rosenzweig, Pierre Missac. Again and again of Gabriel Bounoure, who was always his first reader and sounding board, more: his "life-raft" in a time of intellectual turmoil:

> He read the manuscript of *The Book of Questions* in 1962. And he helped to make almost acceptable to me what in those pages frightened me. He went even further by showing me that, my contradic-

tions being the very substance of my books, trying to avoid them was pointless.

To others, he no doubt speaks of other people, our common friends for example: Claude Royet-Journoud, Anne-Marie Albiach, Jo Guglielmi, Marcel Cohen, Emmanuel Hocquard, Didier Cahen.

•

Commentary by its very nature draws attention to the process of signifying. Reduced to a formula it could be written "A means B." Within the commentary, metaphor doubles, compacts the process: we have a signifier that stands for a signified that in turn stands for, is identified with, another signified. A is B is (talked about in terms of) C. Density. Layers and layers.

Yet transparent.

No single commentary, no single metaphor becomes central. Question follows upon question, commentary upon commentary, metaphor upon metaphor. They are emptied of particularity, are absorbed into whiteness.

It is the metaphors that make me aware of this. At the time I began translating the *Livre des Questions* I was busy pushing metaphors *out* of my poems. Not altogether out, but into the *structure*. So I had, at first, a somewhat allergic reaction to what seemed sheer reveling in analogy. But once you use metaphors in such profusion you subvert their function. The metaphors no longer link just two terms. They change rapidly, range across semantic fields and logical borders, dunes shifting with the wind.

> Childhood is a piece of ground bathed in water, with little paper boats floating on it. Sometimes, the boats turn into scorpions. Then life dies, poisoned, from one moment to the next.
>
> The poison is in each corolla, as the earth is in the sun. At night, the earth is left to itself, but, happily, people are asleep. In their sleep, they are invulnerable.
>
> The poison is the dream.

Childhood, a place of life, fertility, play. The toys can turn poison. In the second paragraph, the poison is no longer in the scorpion, but in flowers. No difficulty yet. I see the parallel: beautiful, loved things contain the possibility of hurt.

However, the poison in the flower is likened to the earth in the sun. Suddenly poison and earth are parallel, whereas the beginning gave us a piece of earth as metaphor for childhood, as what is threatened by poison rather than poison. The relation of poison and earth in the two paragraphs is diametrically opposed. Not only do the images range from toy to animal to plant to geology, but their logical relation changes. The metaphors cannot be organized into a system where their elements would always correspond to the same concepts.

Yet there is a certain consistency of thought that becomes clear with "the poison is the dream." The poison is the element of libido, of anarchy, potentially destructive freedom present in play, in nature, and can at least be imagined on the cosmic level. But this coherence is created by strangely sliding images and relationships.

Even when the relation of terms does not change, the images change with breathtaking rapidity. In the space of one page we find a conversation compared first to a glass of wine, a drink at the sources of the soul, a boat in the raging sea, a horse, a tree, a bee (these last three connected by the image of the circle: the horse in a circus, the rings of the tree, the bee living around its honey-probe), and finally an apple.

The richness undermines itself. It is as if Jabès piled image on image in order to exorcise it. If everything is like something else, no one similarity means anything. We are left with the *gesture* of analogy rather than one specific analogy.

Gesture of analogy. Gesture of commentary: "There is no rest in the kingdom of resemblances."

"Pure" analogy. "Pure" commentary. Gestures. Like "shifters" or "empty signs," they expose the limit of signification. More fundamentally than the statements about silence do. Indices rather than symbols. But what do they point at?

Gershom Scholem: for the Kabbalist everything is endlessly correlated with everything else, everything mirrors everything else, with the result that symbols signify nothing in themselves, "but make something transparent which is beyond all expression."

What Edmond Jabès makes transparent is not the numinous—in spite of the frequency of the word "God." It is the structure of language, of signification. He makes us aware of the imaginary line between signifier and signified by constantly crossing it. And the line between symbol and index. So that at the limits of signification language is made to *show* itself.

Maybe this *is* the numinous.

"Language is the new Spiritus Mundi!" (Marjorie Perloff).

Or, to bring it back down to earth: Language is made to show itself as taking place, as instance of discourse. As Jakobson says of "shifters" (e.g., pronouns), "their meaning cannot be defined without a reference to the message."

> The articulation—the shifting— . . . is not from the nonlinguistic (tangible indication) to the linguistic, but from *langue* to *parole*. *Deixis*, or indication . . . does not simply demonstrate an unnamed object, but above all the very instance of discourse, its taking place. The place indicated by the *demonstratio*, and from which alone every other indication is possible, is a place of language. Indication is the category within which language refers to its own taking place.
>
> *(Giorgio Agamben)*

Adolfo Fernandez-Zoïla has seen this: Jabès does not aim to create concepts linked by a "logos"; his "invention bears on the production of language itself."

•

When Gershom Scholem comes up in conversation, Edmond always comments on his love of words.

"That's what he has in common with the Kabbalists. Only, he calls it philology."

•

Keith and I are staying in rue de l'Epée de Bois. As we struggle out of bed, Edmond and Arlette are already coming back from the market, netbags full of fruit, cheese, bread. Edmond has precise requirements: the best *crèmerie* is on rue Monge, just off the square. For meat: the butcher at the corner of rue Mouffetard and Passage des Postes. If you buy melons get Cavaillon.

The toilet does not flush well. *"Olàlàlàlàlàlà."* Edmond is on his knees trying to fix it. And succeeds, proudly.

"If I were not a writer I would be a plumber."

We agree that the two occupations have much in common. To keep the language flowing or the water, keep the connections, the pipes in good repair.

The first time Emmanuel Hocquard comes to Jabès's apartment Edmond is also on all fours trying to repair something: *"Olàlàlàlàlàlà."*

Emmanuel starts it, and soon we all comment on our problems: *"Olàlàlàlàlàlà,* as Edmond Jabès would say."

•

Edmond detests Chirac, who at this point is mayor of Paris. If he has to mention him, it is infallibly, "Chirac, *ce salaud.*"

We are up early because Solange is coming to clean the apartment.

"No mail?" Edmond asks her.

"Oh," she jokes, "there was a letter from the mayor, but knowing how you feel about him I tore it up immediately."

Another day, Edmond gleefully shows us a cartoon. Chirac is holding an open book. His advisors in the background look worried. Several frames later, Chirac slams the book shut on a fly. General relief: We almost thought he was reading!

At Cerisy, Edmond is asked why there is no *gros rire,* no belly laugh in his work. He replies, that it is, instead, in his life: "I love to laugh, I love to tell stories, I love to joke. It is a way of escaping anxiety. . . ."

Or, if not escaping, at least putting a momentary distance between himself and his anxiety. It is also his substitute for small talk.

•

Keith and I are coming back to the apartment just as Edmond explains to his granddaughter Brigitte, then an impish twelve year old:

"This isn't a word. It doesn't exist."

She looks stricken. "It doesn't exist? That makes me sad."

Brigitte loves teasing her grandfather. She also demands an explanation of our presence and is doubtful when we are described as friends:

"If you are friends *pourquoi vous ne vous tutoyez pas*?"

Rather than try to answer we take her suggestion and go on to the familiar form of address.

•

It takes time before Edmond and Arlette tell us of their difficult first years in Paris. Edmond's initial job was in an art gallery owned by a friend. Edmond gradually realized that it was a sinecure: the income of the gallery did not justify his position. He appreciated the help, but resigned. Then worked in a company that produced advertising films. Writing on little pieces of paper while taking the métro to work, while traveling between Milan, Frankfurt, and Paris.

Arlette first worked as a secretary for the publisher Pierre Seghers, taking shorthand at night. However, the health center she had founded and run in Cairo qualified her to set up a service supervising the health of researchers at the Orsay Institute of Nuclear Physics, which would remain her job until retirement.

•

Even when his time is his own, later, Edmond Jabès works in snatches, in fragments. No matter where, in cafés, in the métro, while walking, at dinner, on little bits of paper, on matchbooks, napkins, in his mind.

•

Francis Bacon fascinates Edmond.

"What do you see in him?" I ask. "I cannot stand him."

"He has a force that is almost overwhelming. He is all violence, paroxysm, vertigo. And in his disfigured faces you have the very upsetting truth of the face."

In his essay on the painter: "Here the scream is the whole figure become scream; elsewhere, laughter is a monster turned laugh."

Does he find the screams of Sarah, of Israel, in these paintings?

•

When we read in Buffalo, in 1978, Raymond Federman takes us to the Albright-Knox-Gallery. Edmond is ecstatic in the Clyfford Still room. Suddenly the fatigue of traveling is gone. He cannot get enough of the huge abstractions. Again, he speaks of force, violence. "A bit like Nicolas de Staël, but much more powerful." This I understand better. Abstract painting with its relations of balance and movement, space empty and filled, seems so much closer to his own sentences.

Edmond would have liked a reproduction of a Still painting on the cover of *The Book of Shares* (though he is happy with Edward Ranney's photograph).

But I suspect this is a concession to American publishers, who always press for a cover image. Five years earlier, when Tree Books prepares to publish *Elya*, his first book in English, Edmond Jabès is horrified at the idea of a Hebrew letter as cover ornament. He quotes me his reply to David Meltzer, which he even wrote in English to be sure he was understood:

> As for the cover I wish to have just the title and my name, without any graphic material. No image or hebrew letters. No graphic goes

with my books and my books can't afford any graphic. The title must appear as if printed in the void.

His French books continue to have plain—void—covers.

•

In Providence, Rabbi Braude's wife, Pen, asks us to bring Edmond Jabès by their house, which is just around the corner.

Keith has recorded the event:

When we got there, Braude was not, but Pen assured us he soon would be. Meanwhile, we sat down: the Jabèses, Rosmarie, Pen, and . . .

But no, she said to me, I can't sit *there*—that's the Rabbi's chair. I found another.

Braude came home, sat in his chair, gave the impression that he wasn't expecting company—or perhaps was unaware that there was company. Pen, however, kept the conversation going.

"Do you ever feel," she asked Edmond, "like the Wandering Jew?" Since Edmond was, uncharacteristically, at a loss for words, I pointed out that the Wandering Jew is, not a Jewish, but a Christian story. As I heard myself say this, it sounded gauche, but—the silence continuing—I went on to claim that we all feel alien sometimes, that my mother (*for instance*) described herself in terms of the great speckled bird. . . .

And it turned out that the Rabbi was, after all, listening.

"Great speckled bird?" he said, as if doubting his ears.

But all that bothered him was the translation. Oh yes, the King James version, he realized, uses that expression, but it has been shown—although the sacred text does *seem* to speak of such a bird—nevertheless, in Palestine, at the time of the prophets, there *was no such bird*.

He suggested that the Hebrew in question may refer to a sort of *hyena*. (My poor mother.) And now, he looked over at Edmond and asked himself,

"Jabès. Jabès. What does that name mean?"

I stuck my foot in again by noting that, in the Old Testament, it is said to mean *he will cause pain* (a derivation which Rosmarie, while translating—only while translating—finds convincing). Braude, to my amazement, pooh-poohed the idea.

"Impossible," he said, going off to his library to consult authorities.

Over the next hour, he came up with many conjectures, one as likely as another. He appeared happy, engaged in these speculations, and finally sorry to see us go.

Later that evening, Rabbi Braude calls. He calls again the next day and, at widening intervals, for several weeks. Each time it is to report that he has worked out another etymology, something else the name Jabès *might* mean.

•

This same year, it is 1986, we read at the University of Massachusetts in Amherst, awkward to get to by train or bus from Providence. If I remember right, we had to head elsewhere the next day.

Ray Ragosta takes the day off from work to drive us. Ray's first book of poems is about to be published. He has been agonizing about the title. He always has enormous difficulty making a decision—so much so that he would like to be Pope: at least, if he reached a decision it would be infallible. After a good laugh at this, Edmond points to a line in one of the poems:

" 'The act proves untenable.' Here is your title."

At the university, I tell this to the snob who treats Ray as "the driver" and see him become respectful, even a little envious of such attention.

It is getting late when we head back. Edmond realizes Ray must be tired and, for the entire three hours of the drive, the master storyteller tells jokes, pausing only for me to translate—and for our laughs.

Keith remembers one of them:

A very rich old Jew is dying. He calls for a Catholic priest.

The priest is puzzled at being called to the deathbed of the Jew, but comes quickly. He finds the man indeed at the extreme, so weak that his voice is faint. The priest must lean down to hear the Jew's last words, marveling at what he thinks must be a miraculous conversion.

The dying Jew tells the priest he wishes him to witness his last will, his final bequests. The priest joyfully agrees.

There are gifts to be left to every member of the family. The priest takes all this down, hurriedly, knowing the big legacies come last.

The voice is fainter. The priest has to lean closer. He feels the Jew's breath on his face.

Some Jewish charities are funded. The priest finds the amounts over-generous, but yes . . . go on, go on.

And finally, the bulk of the estate is to go . . . to the local synagogue.

The priest is stunned.

But why? . . ." he stammers. "Why did you call *me* here? Would you not have found it more suitable to have called in a rabbi?"

"A rabbi?" the Jew says—the priest, hearing him with difficulty, leaning closer. "A rabbi!? . . .

"And me with cholera!"

•

Jokes. Anecdotes. These I can talk about. I cannot talk about his long hours of solitary work, alone with language, with the blank page, the space between impulse and formulation. And with his dead. I cannot talk about his dark hours, his wounds. His books do.

•

In "Mirror and Scarf," one of my favorite chapters in *The Book of Yukel*, the closeness of sound in the two title words, *miroir* and *mouchoir*, sparks a breathtaking meditation on the face as reflection rather than flesh. In English, it is less convincing that "Mardohai Simhon claimed the *scarf* he wore around his neck was a mirror" until, at Simhon's death, a large *scar* is discovered under the scarf. Reflection always comes back to a wound. It both has its origin in a wound and circles it like a scarf-mirror.

Of course the chapter does not end with the anecdote. Rabbis, ever ready with interpretation, pick up the thread:

> "A double mirror [Reb Alphandery said] separates us from the Lord so that God sees Himself when trying to see us, and we, when trying to see Him, see only our own face."

"Is appearance no more than the reflections thrown back and forth by a set of mirrors?" asked Reb Ephraim. "You are no doubt alluding to the soul, Reb Alphandery, in which we see ourselves mirrored. But the body is the place of the soul, just as the mountain is the bed of the brook. The body has broken the mirror."

Reality and appearance. Man and God. Body and soul. And of course, this relation again resembles the basso continuo, the interdependence and enmity of writer and word, book and word. The book kills the word whose place it is, the word which gives it a voice. Voice and soul: two avatars of breath.

"The brook," continued Reb Alphandery, "sleeps on the summit. The brook's dream is of water, as is the brook. It flows for us. Our dreams extend us."

A characteristic move: Jabès leaves the mirror and instead picks up the comparison which had seemed mere ornament. Move from image to image. The mirror's substance has changed from glass to night to soul to water to dream, for "the dream of the source is water," the dream is again a reflecting substance. The images seem to cancel each other out, but the end turns back to the beginning. And other facets of the seemingly abandoned metaphor turn up.

As if developing one image would be a straight line with its illusion of continuity and false confidence. A multitude of images encircles the elusive prey. The larger the prey the more signs needed to surround it.

"Do you not remember this phrase of Reb Alsem's: 'We live out the dream of creation, which is God's dream. In the evening our own dreams snuggle down into it like sparrows in their nests.'

"And did not Reb Hames write: 'Birds of night, my dreams explore the immense dream of the sleeping universe.' "

Man is living God's dream of creation, man is a reflection of God. We are turning back to the anecdote where the face is a reflection. Again in the background, the book as reflection of its creator. Mirrors multiply reflection ad infinitum. Our dreams: dreams within a dream. Now contained within us, now free to explore. Always ambiguous the relation of containing and contained.

> "Are dreams the limpid discourse between the facets of a crystal block?" continued Reb Ephraim. "The world is of glass. You know it by its brilliance, night or day."
>
> "The earth turns in a mirror. The earth turns in a scarf," replied Reb Alphandery.

Now the dream has bent back into the literal mirror which is richer for the detour of commentaries. It has added facets, the multiple reflections of a crystal. It is richer by the world since the world is of glass. The world, itself glass and mirror, turns in a mirror, which is a scarf.

> "The scarf of a dandy with a nasty scar," said Reb Ephraim.

Dandy. An unexpected note. The error of reflection: instead of exploring the wound of our existence it may also be used to cover it up—and to show off.

Here the discussion breaks off, and we have to cross one of the blank spaces—breathing spaces—to a different voice, placed in parentheses:

> "Words are inside breath, as the earth is inside time."—Reb Mares

Now we have explicitly returned to the central concern, the word. And it is well that the dimension of time is brought in. It reminds us of the successive unfolding of discourse, its manifold aspects and facets meandering through the manifold earth. This is one of the reasons discourse can never be finished, can never engulf the center (which is eternity) though it contain the whole earth.

> "Whatever contains is itself contained," said Reb Mawas.

Earth and time, scarf and scar, reflection and existence, mirror and wound, dreamer and dream, book and word, body and soul, mountain and brook, God and man, word and breath, and, if we read on, soul and ladder.

Vertigo. The terms shift. The relation of the terms shifts. The richness undermines itself. If everything is like something else, no one likeness means anything. As I have said, we are left with "pure" analogy, the *gesture* of it rather than any one specific analogy. A gesture that makes the terms transparent for the very structure of language, of signification.

In the colloque de Cerisy, Edmond Jabès brings up a parallel from painting:

> I was struck by the fact that if a painter wants to render transparency he adds more colors. Color in itself is opaque: to make it crystalline one has to add a quantity of colors. For the painter, an overload is transparency.. . . .

It is true that he explicitly opposes the way of the writer to the way of the painter:

> . . . for the writer, on the contrary, the more he takes off the quicker he gets to the essential.

But his own practice includes both the stripping down and the overload—and manages to fuse them. And he explicitly equates the "essential" with "transparency," legacy of the desert, of the interdiction of representation. Transparency for the structure of signification—and for its limits: the silence, the infinite, the nothing, all it is not able to hold.

•

The voices Edmond Jabès invented are still with us. Voices to keep us company now that he is not.

A host of imaginary rabbis. They have names (*des noms d'écoute*, "names of listening"), but are not individualized. They are not characters. Not even the shadowy kind of character that Yukel is ("you are a shape moving in the fog. . . . You are the toneless utterance among anecdotal lies"). Most of them do not speak more than once, though a few are allowed to dispute for several pages. Even then they do not really become persons. What they say is not necessarily consistent. They do not represent a position. They are not authorities. Gabriel Bounoure calls them "candidates for presence, but hesitant to quit their status of shadows."

Voices, rather. A chorus. Of commentary and interpretation. Of exchange. A chorus that points to the phenomenon of voice as such or, rather, to the phenomenon of changing voice, changing perspective. In a rhythm of voice—absence of voice—voice. This is why, in the later books, the rabbis, privileged interpreters though they are, disappear. They become absorbed into the white space between paragraphs, between aphorisms.

"White space," says Bernard Noël, "is silent, but not mute, and it produces a resonance whose vibrations let us feel the limits of language—or its song at the edge of disappearance—or perhaps the trajectory of the verbal event. . . ."

•

Whenever Edmond Jabès has finished a book, has given it to Gallimard, he has severe asthma. Then the period between projects, period of not writing, which he calls his Book of Torment. (During which he returns obsessively to the book he has just handed in. "I had planned to work on this text for Skira," he writes me from the seaside, "but that was counting without *Aely* which I still cannot let go.")

Vacation in Brittany, by the sea, helps the asthma, if not the torment. I imagine him walking on the beach. Slowly. Step by step against the resistance of the air and the sand. The sand, the way it runs through our fingers, is a figure for the vanity of words, but this does not stop us from making it into "the beginning of a garden." The sand, which taught Edmond Jabès to let his words shift and move rather than cling to one designation. Edmond looks for faces on pebbles. Gathers pebbles rather than sentences. Pebbles and sentences. And memories in the sand. The desert next to the sea.

•

I admire Jabès's economy. Whenever he writes an occasional text, to introduce a reading, for instance, I find the text reworked, interspersed with more elliptical passages in the next book. Husbanding his writing as he must husband his breath? After his death, there are no *inédits*.

•

In June 1979, Edmond Jabès is invited to the Cambridge Poetry Festival and gets me invited also. In London, who should climb into our train compartment but Gisèle Celan. She has an exhibition of engravings in Cambridge. Edmond introduces me as his translator, who has also translated Paul Celan's "Conversation in the Mountains." Gisèle Celan looks puzzled. I have to admit that it was a pirated publication. The editor, Anthony Barnett, had asked for permission, but it seems a chapbook called *Writings, I* from a journal called The Literary Supplement, Oslo, was below the notice of Celan's literary executor. He never replied. Edmond jumps in:

"Sometimes a professor does not realize how important this kind of small publication is. It's a sign that the poet is alive for the young."

Gisèle generously agrees.

Edmond reads in one of the evening sessions of the festival. Our friend Anthony Barnett is upset to find C. H. Sisson on the same program. He in turn upsets Arlette:

"Sisson is a fascist, an admirer of Charles Maurras. Edmond should refuse to read with him."

As if on cue, Sisson begins with the poem "Maurras Young and Old." I feel Arlette tense next to me. So tense that she cannot take in the poem. There is nothing fascist about it. It describes Maurras on the eves of the two world wars, with a Latin's scorn for the Teutonic *"irruptio barbarorum."* She looks intently at Edmond as he gets ready to go up on stage. He whispers:

"My work will speak for itself."

•

Edmond's trees: the flamboyant and the date tree. His flower: jasmine. At the mere mention its smell envelops me, stronger than all the smells of Paris, takes me back to a leafy cave, even the ground heavy with the scent. Glowworms glimpsed between leaves. Evening as if there were no other time of day.

How astonishing that Germany and Egypt would share a flower.

Most frequent color: white. The page. And black: letters. And the "anxiety of white and black: Gray."

> When a written word turns suddenly from glistening black to gray, it is because the infinite of the page has paled it.
>
> "O transparency!" he said.
>
> And added, more to himself than to the others:
>
> "Transparency, ah, there's the miracle."

Transparency, the legacy of the desert where there is no color, but where the light is large, open, with a transparent quality in which all colors are present at the same time, as possibility. In the desert, Edmond Jabès says to Serge Fauchereau, "nothing is there as simply blue, but as a possibility of blue." And just as piling on color leads to transparency, so "we pile up images and images of images until the last, which is blank, and on which we will agree."

So Edmond Jabès piles metaphor on metaphor and commentary on commentary for a transparency and degree of abstraction that makes us see language as such, language taking place, its structure laid bare, its foundation on nothingness obvious.

•

This transparency and abstraction that Jabès values is not the same as the transparency for concepts which the philosophers would like words to have: "A symbol which interests us *also* as an object is distracting," says Susanne Langer.

It is the "last image" that is blank—as if there could be such a thing. If there could be, it would have to have exhausted and absorbed the totality of possible images and thereby transcend its very nature. It would join the totality of all possible words that makes up the name of God. *Up until* this impossible last image, it is exactly as an object that the word interests Edmond Jabès (and every poet). As a physical body of sound and letters. A body that has its own volume, mass, density, inertia, constants, surface tension, and, most importantly, an electric charge and vectors toward other words, affinities, shared elements.

We may find it uncomfortable that we are sorcerer's apprentices who cannot control the sign system we invented; that language is not necessarily a tool we can simply "use." Notoriously ambiguous, it cannot be reduced to "single vision" or the precision of logic. But it is the mark of a poet to accept the baffling density and the potential of language even as it outstrips the mind, as it "thinks for us."

What writer has not experienced how a rhyme, a rhythm, an assonance "takes over" and makes us say something other than we first intended? We have long had an image for it: the poet "ravished" by the muse as opposed to the *poeta faber.*

To write: "To wait for words that wake our thoughts as they write us."

•

It is the knowledge that our words are our world that makes Edmond Jabès listen so intently to the words, makes him so passionately try to discover "their own law." So the closeness "word : world" is one of the presents the English language gives me. As if tailored for Jabès's work. "Diamond" is as close to "dialogue" as *diamant* and lends sparkle to the facets of conversation. But what of *vérité* and *vertige*, the vertigo of truth, or the *ver* in *vérité,* the worm in truth? I can find only "rue" in "truth." When Reb Ardash is told he suffers from *mal de vérité* I have him suffer from "truthache" and immediately get qualms: this is over the top, too much. But the text continues:

And Reb Ardash said: "It is not always the heart which closes the loop. Sometimes it is the teeth. There are celestial bites which witness God's despair."

"Truth-ache" stays.

Quelle différence y a-t-il entre l'amour et la mort? Une voyelle enlevée au premier vocable, une consonne ajoutée au second.
J'ai perdu à jamais ma plus belle voyelle.
J'ai reçu en échange la cruelle consonne.

What difference is there between love and loss? a fricative taken away, two sibilants added.
I've lost it forever, my lovely v.
I got in exchange the cruelest sound.

Why does there seem to be a close relation between love and death? For Edmond Jabès, it is not because of any evolutionary connection with the amoeba, which literally dies into its offspring. Nor is it only because of the "little death" we experience in orgasm. It is because the two words (in French) have a surprising number of letters in common. But they don't in English.

It is essential to find words in English that overlap at least somewhat in their letters rather than keep "love" and "death." I am fortunate to have "loss" available which shares at least half its letters with "love" and is within the semantic field of "death." True, the description of the difference in English lacks the simplicity of the change from vowel to consonant in the French. Operating with "fricative" and "sibilant" is more technical, cumbersome, and at the same time less precise because I shift to the level of pronounciation by ignoring the mute *e* in "love" while ignoring the fact that the pronounciation of the *o* is not quite the same in "love" and "loss."

What makes up for this is that the text, within two pages, has a passage about the Nazi SS—indeed the cruelest letters, the cruelest sound in a work that is, on one level, about the holocaust.

•

At other times, no gifts of luck or language. I cannot even find an approximation. I finally have to admit defeat and leave the wordplay in French.

> *"Sais-tu, dit-il, que le point final du livre est un oeil et qu'il est sans paupières?"*
>
> *Dieu, il écrivait D'yeux. "D pour désir, ajoutait-il. Désir de voir. Désir d'être vu."*
>
> *Trait pour trait, Dieu ressemble à son Nom et son Nom est la Loi.*

> "Do you know that the final period of the book is an eye," he said, "and without lid?"
>
> *Dieu,* "God," he spelled *D'yeux,* "of eyes." "The D stands for desire," he added. "Desire to see. Desire to be seen."
>
> God resembles His Name to the letter, and His Name is the Law.

Yet the defeat is also an asset. It confronts us with the presence of the other language which might have slipped from our awareness as we read along. It shows us the other language at play as only it can play.

Goethe insisted that translation must respect the untranslatable because in it lie the value and character of a given language. And even if, as Antoine Berman interprets, "the untranslatable is not this or that, but the totality of the foreign language in its strangeness and difference," it is the specific untranslatable moment that allows us a glimpse of this totality.

•

Edmond and I work on the translation. I read him sentences I am unsure of. He never answers my questions directly. He looks at the paragraph and begins to talk around it, to amplify. He gives me additional context. More crucial yet, he allows me additional glimpses of his way of thinking. He continues the commentary, the main procedure of the book, beyond the book, up to the border between the two languages where the translation, yet another commentary and interpretation, germinates. He, as always, in and out of the book, allows the words to lead to other words, to couple, to go where their passionate desire, *les élans de leur désirs d'amants*, pushes them.

How I wish I had a record of these sessions. But they would not have been the same. Their record is in the translations.

They also confirm my sense that the "unit" of translation is the whole work, not Walter Benjamin's single word. (An idea, let me note, that he did not follow in his practice.) What matters is not so much the solution of particular problems—puns, for instance. It is true that these salient points are most vulnerable to the action of translation. But it is possible to have brilliant equivalents for puns and still miss the tone or the rhythm of the work, the "tempo of its style, of its metabolism," as Nietzsche characterized the most difficult aspect of a work to translate.

I hold with Haroldo de Campos that translation, "transluciferation," must first "dissolve the Apollonian crystallization of the original text back into a state of molten lava." The fluidity in this image comes close to the essential working of the process, although on the conscious level there are hundreds of small decisions. Thinking in terms of the whole work, you can approximate what the original does, perhaps not in the same place, but elsewhere.

Curiously, this is extremely close to Wilhelm Dilthey's notion of interpretation, which

> sets about the task of uncovering the meaning of a text by re-creating the whole process of the genesis of that text. The conceptual premiss behind it is Aristotle's distinction between *ergon* and *energeia*: Interpretation of a work, as Dilthey understands it, consists in "translating the *ergon*—the completed object—back into the *energeia* that brought it forth.

Dilthey had a psychological slant I do not altogether share. He wanted to get at the man behind the work (still a widespread bias); whereas, in translating, I want to get at the way the germ of the work is embedded in its language.

Curiously also, as the work dissolves back into this prior, molten, potential state, my previous readings seem to dissolve along with it. Not altogether, obviously, or I could not approach this state. But passages I thought I understood are suddenly incomprehensible again. And I find myself consulting the dictionary for the simplest, most familiar words, words I "know perfectly well," but which suddenly plunge me into a panicked feeling of total ignorance.

•

Edmond Jabès's road to silence is not minimalism. He is not paring his words down to a minimum, but circling, encircling. A deeper and deeper plunge of involution. He lays siege to silence.

There is silence and silence. Hans-Georg Gadamer has called silence the "third dimension" of all utterance: everything said "refers backward and forward to what is unsaid. . . . And only when what is not said is understood along with what is said is an assertion understandable." But Gadamer's "unsaid" is not an ultimate silence like Jabès's, but merely motivation and context. It is a space for the utterance, not an ultimate limit, a threat of non-space.

Jabès's silence is existential. It is the ground we write on ("We can write only on this silence"). It is "other," inhuman. It threatens us who are defined by language, by the word. But it also challenges us to assert ourselves in our definition. It is our ultimate motivation to speak and in speaking to assert ourselves against the nothingness of silence.

We write in order to deny (*nier*) the nothing (*rien*) that is God, Edmond Jabès repeats.

When Jabès defines writing as a translation from silence ("which has formed the word") into more silence ("silence of the book: a page read") we know he is also talking about our lives. But it is the words that make the silence perceptible. They reduce it, but only in this reduction can it be read: "Writing is an act of silence, allowing itself to be read in its entirety."

The unsaid behind the text: first loss. What is said in the text and rendered unsaid by translation: double loss. And perhaps also a "fortunate fall" that makes us doubly aware of the illegible behind the words?

Edmond Jabès's challenge to the writer is to engage, through the nearly infinite space of language, in a dialogue with its negative, our final limits: silence, the void, or, if you like, our metaphor for these: God. The challenge to the translator is to engage, through the limited space of a text, in a dialogue with the tension between two languages, a tension that in its gaps, lacks, in its non-overlap, non-identity, constantly points toward these same limits.

•

I admire Edmond's confidence. When I ask him,

"What are the "four silver watchtowers" *(vigies)* on the scroll of the Torah that you talk about on page seventy-nine of the *Livre des Questions*?" he begins talking about the staffs the scroll is fastened to, but then stops himself:

"No, this isn't it, there are only two, not four."

We talk about Dante's fourfold interpretation.

"But why 'towers'?"

Finally, he dismisses the problem:

"I am sure I had something precise in mind, but it's a long time since I wrote this text. . . ."

•

Edmond and Claude go for a walk in the zoo of Le Jardin des Plantes. Edmond wants to show Claude the gorillas because, he says, they copulate almost without interruption. But it is Sunday, when parents bring their children. The gorillas are in separate cages. There they sit, masturbating. Edmond and Claude watch. The children watch. Then Edmond says sadly:

"Claude, we must come back on a week day."

•

Arlette reports that their daughters are a little jealous of Claude, "the adoptive son." There are moments that indeed have a family feel, when Claude seems to test the affection of Edmond and Arlette. Once, toward the end of a party chez Jabès, Claude and I stand out on the little balcony for a breath of air. A large group of young people come along the street singing. Claude invites them all to come up and join the party. They are hesitant. It is after midnight. He insists. Edmond gets his black look. He is tired. Most of the guests have already left. But when the doorbell rings, he simply explains that it is an error, the party is over.

Keith remembers how Claude tried to convince Edmond of the greatness of Roger Laporte. It was not the first time. Edmond knew the argument and did not want to hear it again. Claude insisted:

"*Fugue*," said Claude, "is a tribute to you," and went through the book, pulling out sentences to prove it.

"*Dans le cas où l'esprit*," he read out, "*fonctionnant comme une machine, aurait indéfiniment exécuté un programme immuable, j'aurais eu, non point la certitude, mais du moins l'espoir, de parvenir, de rectification en rectification, à construire une machine théorique homothéthique de la pratique de l'écriture . . .*"

"That's you," he told Edmond, "that's you. Well . . . maybe not the machine, but . . ."

Edmond was pretending to take notes:

"C'est moi . . .

". . . sauf la machine."

Claude was laughing as much as the rest of us, but really wanted Edmond to believe.

"But Edmond, he's another you."

"I must admit," replied Edmond, "I prefer myself."

There comes a time when Claude takes his distance. But his affection for Edmond never diminishes. He reads at the memorial for Edmond Jabès in spite of a flu and 104 degrees of fever.

•

In the later work, the key words not only engender the book, they become what Felix Ingold has called a "Leitwort style," which holds the text suspended between the discursive and the poetic, creates figures that are at the same time figures of speech and of thought.

Musical prose. Leitmotifs. But with less closure than this might suggest. It is true that we keep coming back to the words Edmond Jabès himself designated as key words: *God, Jew, Law, Eye, Name, Book*. And we could add: *Death, Absence, Threshold, Desert, Word, Dialogue, Mirror, Question*. But it is never just one, never even just one predominant. A theme is sounded, interrupted, another theme enters, grows louder, is interrupted in its turn. Not closing into a fugal structure, but spiraling outward. As if each book had a horizon for its center.

•

In a review, Ammiel Alcalay tells of meeting Edmond and Arlette in the lobby of a Jerusalem hotel. An Egyptian film is showing on the TV.

> Palestinian workers from the hotel sat on the couch, watching and commenting. Neither Edmond nor Arlette could hide their delight at the black-and-white images of their former, Cairene life on the screen. Soon they were among the workers, gossiping away in Arabic about the famous stars.

This reminds me of the way Edmond looks when he talks of Oum Kalsoum, when he tries to describe the way her songs bring up ancient lamentations. How suddenly Egypt seems in his eyes. His phrase comes back to me:

"She had *tarab*."

"What is *tarab*?"

"It's untranslatable. It's ecstasy. Intoxication of the senses. But more so."

I do not expect ever to hear this singer, but here she is, in November 1998, on the French-German TV channel "Arte," holding on to her famous handkerchief. Elderly people reminisce, Naguib Mahfouz among them:

"She had *tarab*."

Otherwise Arlette's music is Bach, whereas Edmond feels close to Boulez, Stockhausen, and especially Nono, who reciprocates the attention and sets a Jabès text in his "Découvrir la subversion—hommage à Edmond Jabès." This piece has been recorded by the Arditti Quartett in 1987.

Music that questions. Sequences of notes that are not melody. Wide intervals that feel to Edmond like the breaks, the white spaces in his own work. A rhythm precise, but not a beat, suspended arcs, breathed.

Jean Frémon is right that Edmond *could* have said "I have little taste for melody (but for timbre, tessitura, silence, listening)."

•

We could not be at Edmond Jabès's funeral. I imagine his body. Thin. Thin. A white flame in the black flame of death. Now a simple plaque in the Columbarium of Père Lachaise:

Edmond JABÈS
1912–1991
Ecrivain
—
Arlette JABÈS
née COHEN
1914–1992

All writers want the word to be flesh. The flesh of a bird, so it can take wing. Now the flesh has become words. And the words live among us.

I am surprised to learn Edmond was cremated. He had talked of giving his body to science. I don't dare ask Arlette, who, I know, has gotten much flak about the cremation from Jewish friends. I ask his daughter Viviane. Yes, she laughs, he changed his mind. He saw on TV that one use of such bodies is to strap them into cars for accident simulation.

C'est trop fatigant, he said, "much too tiring," and gave up on the idea.

Exploded book. Exploded body. Writing as a bomb.

•

I read Gershom Scholem's essay, "The Oral and the Written": "The *Midrash Konen*, dealing with cosmogony, repeats that the pre-existent Torah was written in black fire on white fire." Then he quotes a fragment attributed to one of the very first Provençal Kabbalists, Isaac the Blind, that describes the pre-existent Torah:

> In God's right hand were engraved all the engravings [innermost forms] that were destined some day to rise from potency to act. . . . This formation is called the concentrated, not yet unfolded Torah, the Torah of Grace. . . . Two engravings were made in it, the written Torah and the oral. The form of the written Torah is that of the colors of white fire, and the form of the oral Torah has colored forms as of black fire.

Shock of recognition. This is the passage Edmond keeps talking about one whole summer. *What the black of fire wrote on the white of fire*. He speaks at first as if for himself, as if preliminary, searching for words, thinking. Or perhaps reading. ("We always start out from a written text and come back to the text to be written, from the sea to the sea, from the page to the page." But gradually the words seem to turn outward, address me, whoever is in the room, a soundboard to test formulation. Days later, the phrase comes again, this time it's "what the black of fire *carved*." And it is surrounded by different words. This origin of the word must mean that fire remains inside the word. It cannot die in the word it has written. And what is fire unless desire.

Later, in *The Book of Margins*, in the "Letter to Jacques Derrida on the Question of the Book," I find: "Fire, virginity of desire" and:

> I came across the answer proposed by a kabbalistic rabbi . . . an answer that I would divert from its original mystical sense and submit

> to your literal reflection: that the Book is "what the black of fire carves into the white of fire." Black fire on white fire. Endless consuming of sacred parchment and profane page given over to signs, as if what is consigned—co-signed—to writing were only a play of flames, fire of fire, "word-fires," you said in a recent interview. Confidence in what dies purified to be reborn of the desire for purifying death, thanks to which words add to their own the readability of a time advanced to the "deferred" reading, which we now know is the reading of all reading; time forever preserved within abolished time.

Now the tentative speech has turned outward for good, has been fixed, A movement of the mind has become language, visible. It has—temporarily—lost the voice. But reading, even silent reading, will revive it. The sentences have gained in precision what they have lost in immediacy. But they still carry a trace of halt and hesitation, of turning to another, of making space for reply.

Not that this explains anything about the genesis of the text. I am excited to have been present at a moment that marked the process, but I am pinpointing only a seed, an impulse. *How* the experience, "lived" or verbal, is transformed into the text we cannot know. Not even while we write. If we knew, the text would show it. Better to trust to the sudden detours, hidden alleys, unexpected corners imagination takes us to.

•

I have come to Paris by myself. I am staying with Edmond and Arlette, but occasionally go out without them. In the morning, Edmond asks:

"When did you get in last night?"

I have definitely been adopted.

•

Edmond gets a letter saying: We are cousins. It seems you have written a very important work. Please send me the seven volumes of *The Book of Questions*.

Edmond is annoyed. He has never met this man, never heard from him before. On the other hand, they *are* related. What should he do? Maybe he could send him just one volume?

Much later, we are talking about family:

"Edmond, what did you finally do about the cousin who wanted the seven volumes of *The Book of Questions?*"

"Oh, I just waited three months and then wrote him that I was astonished I hadn't gotten any word of thanks!"

•

I am puzzled by a phrase about the Jew's back "bent by the stone," *vouté par la pierre*. Edmond seems puzzled too, looks at the paragraph and laughs:

"It is a misprint. It should be *vouté par la prière*, back bent from bending down in prayer."

But then adds: "I don't mind the typo. You could think of all the stones thrown at Jews over the centuries. They also have bent our back."

•

When people try to see Edmond Jabès's work as coming from one theory or another, Structuralism, Lacanism, Saussurian linguistics, he brushes it aside with *c'est vécu*, "it is lived, experienced." So obviously true. So obviously false. Of course writing has to come out of our life. But is reading not also part of living?

Still, Edmond Jabès writes *aphorisms* that by definition, at least the *Britannica*'s definition, come out of experience. He does not write *axioms*, not self-evident truths that appertain to pure reason.

> If there is theory, it came out of a questioning which touches on man as much as on the word, on man at the moment of writing, when he becomes words. . . . The supposed author. . . . remembers today his slow progress in the book and how he was rejected by it: evicted from

a privileged place where his freedom played at the expense of his existence.

When my first book of poems was published I did not want to be classed as an "academic poet" and insisted there be nothing about university training or Ph.D. in the jacket copy. I did not realize that, for a woman, there was a worse category: the "housewife poet." Some press release must have had additional information because I got two kinds of reviews: the housewife treatment and the respectful ones, which invariably mentioned my academic credentials.

•

Edmond Jabès eagerly awaits each new book by Samuel Beckett. He feels a great affinity with Beckett's project. They both keep digging deeper and deeper in their chosen path, their questioning. Both are unafraid of last things. Though Beckett rather settles on the next-to-last, the dailiness of lack, of stripping away—in great detail. Whereas Jabès seems perched on the very edge where detail gives way to abstraction. And, of course, there is Beckett's flatness, expression strictly rationed, whereas for Edmond Jabès the desert was so overwhelming an experience that his Void and Nothingness are as grandiose, even numinous, as God ever was.

•

We are walking by the paulownias of the Place de la Contrescarpe. Here and there, grass peeks out between the paving stones. Astonishing in the city, the place of passage where nothing takes root.

Edmond asks: Tell me about your life. Flustered, I come out with what happens to be on my mind: my sister had just sent me a letter my mother had written to her mother shortly after my birth. She was desperate because I refused her breast. I am confounded that our conflict began in my infancy. Then I am mortified to have spoken of this. I imagine that Edmond, asked to tell about his life, would begin: there is a passage in the Talmud . . .

But he speaks of the night his sister died. And he, twelve years old, the only one with her.

This is the only time he speaks at length of his family. He rarely mentions his parents, though he felt close enough to his mother to entitle an early book, *Maman*. He never talks about his older brother, who committed suicide in 1964. They edited a magazine together, in 1930, when he was eighteen and his brother twenty-six. It was called *Alliance franco-egyptienne* and tried, like many other early efforts of Edmond's, to hold together the two halves of his heritage that were already coming apart.

•

"The illegible lies in wait where legibility falters."

•

The day we hear of Edmond's death Keith and I keep huddling, clinging to each other.

Arlette writes that he died napping after dinner, with two new books next to his chair: one by Leiris, the other Keith's *A Ceremony Somewhere Else,* translated by Françoise de Laroque.

Edmond dies in January 1991. It takes me till August to resurface in the present. August, when we prepare to leave for a year in England. January to August, a period that parallels, doubles the months of first getting to know him, exactly twenty years earlier.

The slopes of the mountain can still get some sun when the valley is already dark. But it is less warm. I reread Edmond Jabès's body of work. But the real body is no more.

"Your body is a book of thoughts that cannot be read in its entirety."

•

When Edmond Jabès comes to the States, in spring 1981, I am teaching at Tufts University. Our reading there is ironically sponsored by the German department. French has pleaded lack of funds, but Sol Gittleman, head of German and Slavic Studies, is enthusiastic about the books. After the reading, several professors of French come to thank Sol.

As always, the "battle of the salt" provides much entertainment. Wherever we eat, Arlette makes sure Edmond is served salt-free meals. She is fierce. He, however, makes his way to the buffet and sneaks a bit of savory polenta, an olive, a potato chip before she can catch up with him.

Or he confounds his hostesses: "Do you know why salt-free food is given to the old? It's so we won't regret life."

There is an early casualty. While I am teaching a class, Harriett Watts takes Edmond and Arlette to Boston University. Arlette suggests a taxi. Harriett insists it is not very far. But there is the bag. It is heavy to carry.

Edmond's heart condition does not allow him such exertion, and Arlette watches fiercely that he does not. As fiercely as she insists on salt-free meals. Overeagerly, Harriett insists on walking and on carrying the bag—and hurts her back.

We wonder: is this a bad omen? There are big stakes on this tour. Wesleyan University Press has a new director. We hope that our reading at Wesleyan will persuade her to continue publication beyond the first three volumes of *The Book of Questions*. Jeannette Hopkins is both charmed by Edmond and impressed by the work. Wesleyan continues to publish not only the next four volumes of *The Book of Questions,* but also the three volumes of *The Book of Resemblances*; it publishes also *The Book of Dialogue, A Foreigner . . . ,* and a Jabès Reader: *From the Book to the Book.*

At the moment when Wesleyan University Press had accepted the first volume of my translation, but not yet signed the contract with Gallimard, I got a call from senior editor Bill Bueno:

"You've had a narrow escape."

The Press budget was cut by fifty percent. The Press wanted to drop all unsigned contracts, but at the meeting with the faculty advisory board, Jan Miel made an impassioned speech that *The Book of Questions* must be kept on.

Then Bueno asked me to waive my translator's fee.

Jan Miel's field is Pascal. He is also very interested in Derrida, Foucault, Lacan (some of whose essays he translated). I convinced him to read Jabès by quoting Derrida's statement of 1972: "Since then [i.e., 1963, the publication of *The Book of Questions*] nothing has taken shape 'in current literary production,' as you say, that does not have its precedent somewhere in the text of Jabès."

Now, five years later, Edmond meets his champion. The day after the reading, we go to a restaurant that is half an hour's drive from Middletown. Edmond manoeuvers to ride alone with Jan. I am curious about their conversation because I suspect that Jan has not read as much of Jabès's work as Edmond assumes. Jan refuses to be drawn on this question.

•

Edmond and Arlette go by themselves to a "round table" at Princeton. They are introduced to Susan Sontag.

"Are you a writer?" Edmond asks.

•

Back in Providence, the rabbi at Brown University (a man much younger and more worldly than Rabbi Braude) has a dinner for the poet, before the reading.

Keith remembers:

> It was pleasant enough, but halfway through the meal, Edmond was visibly in pain, having a hard time breathing. We ran him by the house, where he had asthma medicine in his suitcase.
>
> He was fine then, and the reading went well.
>
> "He tends to get an attack like this," Arlette whispered to me, "whenever he gets near a rabbi."
>
> Rabbi Braude (to whom Edmond developed no allergy) came to

see him the next summer in Paris. Arlette brought out large glasses of lemonade.

On this extremely hot day, Braude is happy to see lemonade, but insists that a small amount of it be put in a glass for him, since otherwise he might not be able to drink it all and some would be wasted.

"Our religion," he says, "teaches us that waste is wrong."

In smaller glassfuls, he has no trouble finishing the pitcher.

•

The summers we spend at 7 rue de l'Epée de Bois, Keith and I are conscious of crowding the small apartment. We try to make ourselves thin. Keith haunts the bookstores. I work in rue Calvin where the *Bureau d'acceuil* for foreign professors has made available a room plus typewriter. Or sit and read in the café of the Mosque, the coolest place with the slowest service, perfect for a summer afternoon.

Edmond, with infinite tact, pretends to be annoyed:

"What is this? You are never here."

•

Now, eight years after Edmond Jabès's death, I am walking toward rue de l'Epée de Bois from rue Monge. I have long meant to look up *mercitur* on the cartouche at the corner: *Fluctuat nec mercitur.* Should it not be *mergitur*? Part of the letter g worn off? I lean for a moment against against the red and buff brick of the Centre de la Santé, to look at the facade of the house opposite No. 7, to remind myself of the view from the Jabès balcony. The ironwork is lovely, ornate, and there are the two stone roses I remember.

No. 7. The curtain blowing out the window.

The past fills this street, but the street takes no notice. The Café de la Poste is still here, but the rest has changed. "Linéa Store," a nutrition councelor where I knew a pizza parlor. "Le continent: Objets du monde" with its African clothes and statues has replaced the

Arab grocery store. I walk up the sidewalk ramp to the toy store I remember, but it is closed. It's Monday.

•

Clochards under the Pont Neuf, with a trash fire under a tin of food. Paris has its nomads.

•

A photo of a demonstration in Paris. The French government is trying to deport all illegal immigrants, all *sans-papiers*. Documentary film-makers are the first to draw attention to the hardship this is causing. Writers, artists, and translators are quick to join in. Many translators feel that they, as mediators between cultures, are particularly concerned, says Rosie Pinhas-Delpuech (even though the Translators' Association as a whole does not take an official position). Petitions and appeals appear in newspapers, and now there is a huge demonstration. The Translators' Association is out in force. As a banner, Rosie Pinhas-Delpuech holds up Edmond Jabès's book:

Un étranger
avec, sous le bras,
un livre
de petit format

•

The question of otherness. What is foreign. Most directly in this book, *A Foreigner / Carrying in the Crook / of His Arm a Tiny Book*, Edmond Jabès's response to the increasing racism and intolerance he witnesses in France (and elsewhere) during his last years. Here he pinpoints the basis of intolerance: our craving for unity, for One truth, One religion, One culture, One identical image of ourselves.

> As if . . . the soul vibrated only to one single sound, as if the mind could get excited only once.

Whereas: "when we say 'I' we already say *difference*." And it is in the encounter with the stranger that we find our own self, our own strange "I": *L'étranger? L'étrange-je?*

Here is one of the deep reasons why there is no single line of discourse in Jabès's work, but, instead, room for difference and multiplicity, fragments and facets; why he opens language to different perspectives (which according to Handelman "emerge from and displace the dialectical negations of rabbinic and Kabbalistic thinking"); why he opens it to the otherness of silence. It explains why he is fond of paradox, of what goes beyond or against one single doxa, opinion, or truth. As Accursi puts it:

> Reason, Cartesian "common sense," conditions discourse, method, rationality; it permits order, classification, command, and the foundation of thought. It affirms one single and good direction.
>
> The paradox, by contrast shows that sense always goes in two opposite directions at the same time. The two senses do not contradict each other in succession as in Hegelian dialectic . . . they coexist in the same moment and diverge simultaneously. . . . Hence it makes it impossible to know which is the good direction. The paradox hinders one-way thought and common sense.

Edmond tells me the story behind the title, *A Foreigner / Carrying in the Crook of His Arm a Tiny Book*: at the time of the Inquisition, the Marranos, the Christianized Jews of Spain, used to carry a tiny edition of the Old Testament to church, concealed, literally up their sleeve, so that they could touch it, caress it, while making a show of following the mass they were forced to attend.

This story is not told in the book to which it gave its title. With rather typical out-of-phase motion, it appears two years later, 1991, in *Desire for a Beginning Dread of One Single End.*

•

"A stranger twice over," he said, "as author of a book he did not write and reader of a book that writes him. A stranger to the book and to himself."

We write in order to deny (*nier*) the nothing (*rien*) that is God. Again, to write means "to wait for words that wake our thoughts as they write us."

•

As part of the celebration for his seventy-seventh birthday in 1989, Edmond reads from this new book, *Un etranger avec sous le bras un livre de petit format.*

It is a moving performance. He looks frail, a bit tired. His voice is becoming a little brittle, which makes the figure of the foreigner he reads about all the more poignant. Afterwards, I am talking with his daughter Viviane and granddaughter Brigitte, when an acquaintance comes up and asks Brigitte:

"Was Edmond Jabès a jolly grandpa?"

To my surprise she replies:

"Jolly, yes, but not much of a grandpa."

And Viviane, who is so close to her father and his work, confirms that, as a father, too, he had not been very present, his mind always a bit elsewhere, absorbed in his writing. But how often have I heard him say that he felt blessed in his family:

Je suis comblé dans ma famille.

•

The diagrams in *El, or the Last Book*:

NUL L'UN	:	NONE ~~N~~ONE

Curious that both languages show a relation between "one" and "none" on the level of the word. The relation is different. In French, "none" is the reverse of "one"; English, with curious arithmetic, subtracts from "none" to arrive at "one." But this difference in the relation is less important than the fact that the change is small in either language.

A few pages later there is a table where Jabès has crossed out letters to signal the closeness of *livre, libre, lire*—book, free, read. This relation interests him more than, say, that the Latin word *liber* and the French *livre* refer to the layer between the sapwood and the bark of a tree, or that *bouquin* and the English word "book" are both derived from Latin *buxus* or beech, no doubt because beech tablets were used for writing. Though, in *El, or the Last Book*, he uses the former etymology—only to bring it immediately again into his prefered type of relation:

> "The liber, inner bark of the linden, bast or hemp we use to make ropes and mats, but also to write.
>
> "In 'liberty,' there is the word 'liber' rewriting it. Thus the word 'liberty' writes us into the freedom of the word which writes it," he said.

And note that his choice of plants to mention is also governed by the similarity of their French names: *tilleul, teille, ou tille*.

> "Fin *resurgit, pour l'oreille, du mot* Faim. *La fin est affamé," disait-elle.*
> *"Dans les brumes du mot* savoir, *il y a le mot* voir. *Savoir, disait-il, c'est essentiellement voir . . ."*
> *Néant : né en . . .*
> *Privé d'R, la mort meurt d'asphyxie dans le mot.*
> *"Dans le mot* corps, *disait-il, gît le mot* or . . ."
> *Le mot* aérien *est menacé, dans son propre sein, par le mot* rien.
> *L'étranger? L'étrange-je?*

Edmond Jabès listens to the language, thinks along with it and finds that language *is* thought. A more encompassing thought than ours. It can think the unthought. Even the sand of the unthinkable, the "impen*sable*".

> The unthinkable (impen*sable*) is perhaps only the unthought to which has been added its lot of sand *(sable)*.

•

We are en route somewhere in the U.S., in a bus or train. Edmond talks about Beckett. He contrasts him with George Bataille. Bataille is shallow by comparison.

"But he makes up for it in breadth, in scope," I object.

"That's not what is important."

I know he wants me to agree with him because his way is like Beckett's, is to stake out a plot of ground and dig deeper and deeper. I tease him about wanting one single right way, one single hierarchy, after all.

•

We are walking in Providence. The smell of lindens in bloom takes me back to childhood illness with warm linden tea, sounds coming as if through layers of cotton, and a feeling of being immensely far away. Edmond puts a coughdrop in his mouth and drops the wrapper on the sidewalk. Not furtively, with a large gesture. They are rare, the moments that recall the man used to servants. Though he is always "*seigneural*" (Claude's word). The wrapper rises up in a little whirl, along with the dust, and settles again, after a spin on the downwind.

Edmond asks: "When you dream, how do the people look? Do they speak German or English?"

"It depends. Often German."

"Are the houses made of wood, as in Providence?"

"Stone, most often."

"Are there rivers, meadows?"

"A river that doesn't start, maybe doesn't flow. Roads without beginning or end."

"Without beginning or end," he says. "You might be approaching the desert. My dreams are of the desert."

•

As I get closer to Edmond Jabès it seems his inner space is getting larger, so that while I seem to advance, the distance remains always the same.

Just as his eyes seem to come into his face from a larger space, kindle, then travel off again.

But maybe I am myself this distance that separates me from him and, as I seem to get closer, I become more aware of it.

"distance is the place" (Claude Royet-Journoud)

•

In Paris again, we go to see an exhibition of still lifes by Morandi. Edmond is transported by the "explosion of erotism" in the work. I am a bit surprised. The still lifes—bottles in subtle colors—do not strike me as erotic. I can't resist teasing: does he call "erotic" whatever pleases him aesthetically? He speculates that the erotic charge in both production and perception might increase with age and that he is therefore in a better position to appreciate it than I am.

We eat most often in Vietnamese restaurants. At the Grand Pacifique in the early years. After it has folded, in the Village Broca. In both restaurants, Edmond and Arlette are regulars, recognized by the owners, given special treatment. Edmond loves the fine sauces, the flavor of lemon grass. He teaches us to assemble the *rouleau de printemps*. He is particularly fond of a shrimp dish called *Les Demoiselles du Mekong*. We joke about its eroticism.

I think of the glowing red, the intensity of color that announces the departure, the imminent absence of the sun.

Mort rose, moroses méditations du soleil à son déclin.
Rose death, morose meditation of the setting sun.

•

When Edmond is tired he passes his hand over his face as if he wanted to smooth out the wrinkles, ridges in the sand. As if his face too were a desert that has no place, no book.

> "Do you know," he asked, "how grains of sand in the desert sometimes get that greyish hue? It is not the approach of night, but the veil of ashes that covers our futureless books."

•

The lure, the anguish, the pull of the deep. Edmond Jabès builds ladders up into an empty sky. Paul Celan plunges into the Seine. Alain Veinstein digs down into the earth.

> The ladder urges us beyond ourselves. Hence its importance. But in a void, where do we place it?
>
> "I rise, but way up there is my soul trying to rise still higher."

Depth is not a human experience. Both Empiricists and Rationalists assimilate depth of space to size of objects seen in profile. Merleau-Ponty points out that the subject would have to leave his point of view and imagine himself more or less ubiquitous, i.e., *with God's perspective*. Depth is fatal.

•

My new book, *Reluctant Gravities*, has much Jabès in it. Passages on "place," for instance. For a long time I have had to defend my writing against his books. Or thought I had to. Fear of being overwhelmed. I am a little jealous when Keith takes a phrase from my translation and puts it in a poem: "lavish absence." Now I have taken it back.

•

Self-reference has been an epidemic in twentieth century literature ever since the *Faux-Monnayeurs* and *Six Characters in Search of an Author.* Many see it as a closing in, as complete circularity, a "literature of exhaustion." But it is rather an instance of *open form.* The circle cannot close because of its paradoxical nature.

By the time the book about writing the book reaches the reader, the process it shows as unfolding has come to an end. On one level. The reader revives the process.

The paradox of self-reference: The subject that takes itself for its own object, the book that writes about its own process, blurs the line between subject and object, between maker and made, as Maurice Beebe has explained. It makes us refer back and forth between subject and object, between language and meta-language, book and meta-book in an unresolvable oscillation.

When a person speaks about himself we have ways of checking the statements against outside information, against the point of view of others for whom the speaker is only an object, not subject and object at the same time. Within the frame of a literary work there is no "outside," no way of checking. We know we cannot trust what the subject says about itself. But as we try to see "through" the statement to its object, we are thrown back on the statement of the subject because it is all we have to go on.

Rosalie Colie's *Paradoxia Epidemica* sees the paradox as equivocal and dialectic, in opposition to certainty and simple answers. Therefore it is prized in times of multiple and conflicting values like the Renaissance—and our own century, I would add.

Daniel Accursi goes farther. He sees paradox and contradiction as the energy that drives thought:

> Thinking means contradicting yourself permanently. . . . Contradiction is the motor of thought. . . . Thought is by nature crazy, rebellious, polemical, delirious. It progresses only by ambiguity, misconception, nonsense, absurdity, paradox. Contradiction is a machine for creating a plurality of sense.

Indeed, it is the "double vision" of the paradox that makes it a prime instance of what Keats has called *negative capability*: "when man is capable of being in uncertainties, Mysteries, doubts, without any irritable reaching after fact and reason." It is a challenge to closed systems.

A risky form. There is no such thing as a slightly flawed paradox. It either succeeds in juggling its two terms or, with the slightest imperfection, collapses and eliminates itself. Likewise, the books written about their own process of writing have to be *tours de force* or will be trivial.

Paradox marks Jabès's work throughout, from literal paradoxes ("Are we not the image of the void which has no image?" or "My name is in my pain, and my pain has no name" via the paradoxical use of commentary and metaphor up to the macrostructure of self-reference.

Jabès does not simply play the "god game" of reflecting on the world he creates. Nor does he play the negative complement of the god game like Borges's *Circular Ruins* and Beckett's trilogy. I mean the pattern: if I create this world that seems so real then I may in turn be a fiction, the creation of another imagination. This doubt about the reality of the creator posits another creator outside the work or, rather, an infinite series of creators. In this linear chain (a is invented by b, b by c, c by d, etc.) each creator would seem to be "more real" than the created. So "reality," "God," the "original" creator is pushed off into an infinite distance, but is nevertheless postulated and connected with the work we are reading by this chain of successively less powerful creators.

Jabès also has doubts about the reality of the creator. But he does not relate it to a reality (or other fiction) *outside* the work, but to the reality of the words *within* it. Does the author use words or is it, rather, the words that use the author as an instrument to come into being?

The writer as catalyst rather than as a demiurge. A threat to our wishful image of rational man in control of his world?

> The more I care about what I write, the more I cut myself off from the sources of my writing. The more sincere I want to be, the faster I must let the words take over: I cannot refuse to let them exist without me.

> And yet I am at the origin of their existence. I am, therefore, the man who conceived the verbal being which will have a fate of its own on which, in turn, my fate as a writer depends.

A paradoxical state. The writer is at the origin of the words and yet depends on them for his own existence. The writer, on the basis of his material being, creates an immaterial work that continues to exist beyond his material existence.

It is not exactly the logical contradiction of the famous Cretan who says all Cretans are liars. Edmond Jabès is more concerned with origins. Hence the contradiction is in time, a "genetic paradox." Chicken or egg? But it is as equivocal as the truth or falsehood of the Cretan because the two contradictory dependencies, the two contradictory temporal sequences cannot be resolved. They are so balanced that one relation never outweighs the other, that we cannot take one without reference to the other. The relations are infinitely mirrored in one another, as in the logical paradox.

A commentary that invents its own pre-text. A creature that invents his creator. A signifier that invents its signified.

> In creating, you create the origin that swallows you.

> You comment on your commentary and so on and on until you are the great-grandson of your own son.

And most strikingly: "God is sculpted." The human being may be a reflection of God, but God is sculpted, is made. By whom if not us? And if the space of sculpture, three-dimensional space, seems more real than the two-dimensional mirror and its virtual space of reflection, is it not man who gives this reality to God?

At the Colloque de Cerisy, Edmond Jabès says, "the origin is not behind, but before us," is always still to come. Cause becomes the effect of its own effect.

•

Is this mysticism, as Giancarlo Carabelli claims? No doubt Jabès's attitude toward words is rooted in mysticism, in the Kabbalah, where every configuration of letters is an aspect of God's creative power; where everything is contained in the four letters of the name of God; where using any word means actually *reading* the name of God.

And there are many passages that use Neoplatonic-Kabbalistic ideas. Take *El, or the Last Book*, which begins by quoting the Kabbalah: "When God, *El*, wanted to reveal Himself / He appeared as a point." A point that in both traditions expands into creation and contracts again to a point at the end of time. The real title of the book, Edmond always insists, is the fine point in red. The words *El, or the Last Book* are a concession to the publisher. (We happen to be there when Edmond Jabès receives two mock-ups of the cover. One has a fine point, the other a bullet. Which is better? Edmond asks Keith, who declares that the bullet is an image; the fine point, a period, a grammatical marker. "This is exactly what the painter Lars Fredrikson said," Edmond replies. And opts for the period, for "God refused image and language in order to be Himself the point."

Or take:

> God only repeats God: but man? Ah, man also repeats God.

This sounds much like Plotinus's "One" from whose self-contemplation emanate intellect (*nous*) and ideas. The latter are immersed in contemplation, not of themselves, but of the One. Whence emanates the soul immersed in contemplation of Intellect, etc.

But there is a crucial difference. Jabès is no mystic. He is not even a religious writer in the narrow sense. In Jabès, the transcendence is empty. His "God" is a metaphor and does not exist. Man invents God in his likeness so that he can consider himself created by God in His likeness.

On the other hand, Jabès shares the mystics' view that linear logic has its limits, and that beyond those, paradox becomes an epistemological tool. It takes an ambiguity in perception to make us conscious of perception. Much in the same way, a paradox startles us into thinking.

As for the "genetic paradox," Benveniste's examination of utterance and the performative has shown a similar paradoxical, circular interdependence between *langue* and *parole*. *Parole* is not the simple individual application of a preexisting system. Sense and syntax cannot be defined independently of the acts of utterance that it presupposes.

And we have all been caught in the "hermeneutic circle" with its interdependence of detail and whole.

•

In his later years, the Kabbalah is much in Edmond Jabès's mind. I remember mentioning that Louis Zukofsky, in his epic *"A,"* plays on the fact that Columbus discovered America in 1492, the year the Jews were expulsed from Spain. So that it is then that the Spanish Jews begin a migration toward this new continent, albeit with a long detour via Germany, Russia, all of Eastern Europe.

Edmond seems not to be listening. Then, after some silence, begins to talk about the concept of *simsum*, which arose in Lurianic Kabbalism around the time of the expulsion of 1492. The creation occurs when God voluntarily contracts himself into nothingness to make room for the world to emanate from him. A projection of exile onto the cosmic plane.

•

> But for those who are in love with the absolute, obsessed by eternity, turning to God to adore or destroy Him means reaching the depth of human anguish. For we are desperately driven to claim responsibility for the death of God in order to love Him more than ourselves, against ourselves. . . .
>
> Deprived of God in His equivocal death where the creature's fate is a baroque pattern of writing.

I am still (always!) fascinated by the way Edmond Jabès could use the word "God," could engage the whole metaphysical complex. So that translating him becomes a way of "writing" what I cannot write. Would it have worked if he had been a believer? God as metaphor, fine. For what we find as we try to think the unthinkable, know the unknowable—"and screw the inscrutable," as one preacher had it.

> To write as if addressing God. But what to expect from nothingness where any word is disarmed?

> God's being beyond conditions depends on this first and ultimate evidence, the very condition of His freedom from them: *not to be.*

> "Can we be like Him, Who, in His essence, is without likeness?" asked Reb Eliav.
>
> He was told: "Are we not the image of the void which has no image?"

•

The signified is not given. The story is lacking. It comes into being only through its commentary. The signified must be created by its signifier. We must invent a God so that we can be created in His image.

> A double mirror separates us from the Lord so that God sees Himself when trying to see us, and we, when trying to see Him, see only our own face.

The meaning of the double mirror is clear. It embodies the paradox of creating our creator. There is a difference though: God sees "Him*self*," whereas we see only "our *face*." Complete self-knowledge is only possible for a god. We remain with appearance.

Note also that this double mirror completely separates the two planes. If we cannot see God, God cannot see us either. There are two self-contained sets of reflection. But at their midpoint, a maddening vertigo kindles the desire to transcend them. So that God together with His mirror image (man) is a reflection of man aspiring to the condition of godhead, i.e., self-knowledge.

Man's quest is to know himself. The book's quest, to know its process.

•

Man's mirror and instrument of self-knowledge is, above all, language. *Yaël* is the book that openly allegorizes the relation of man and woman as the relation of the writer and the word. Throughout, Yaël, woman and word, has the function of a mirror.

This becomes clear in the writer-narrator's relation to the "other." He is jealous of the "other." Who is this "other?" A rival lover. A rival writer who would also have a relation to the word. But he is more than that. In a scene where the narrator and Yaël make love, the narrator and the "other" fuse:

> Was it me or *the other* embracing her? *The other,* no doubt, whom Yaël always spoke to, always looked at with so much kindness that it hurt me deeply. However, that morning or that night, I do not remember which, something strange happened which I cannot get out of my mind. I was no longer the same. I was no longer myself. I was *the other* or, rather, I finally took his place and was so excited, so grateful to the auspicious hour and the whole world that I lost control and pressed Yaël to myself so long that she collapsed without a sign of life.

We pass rapidly from the identification of the two men (which the writer at first attributes to the woman's imagination) to a different plane where the writer recognizes the word as a mirror that doubles him into "moi" and the sufficiently different "other" that he becomes in his writing: "First, my relations with *the other.* It began with Yaël suddenly turning her eyes from their object to take in a world where I was not." There is an exaltation of insight as well as the pleasure of taking the place of the other in the love scene above. For although "between me and me, Yaël cannot choose," she prefers the other. The word prefers its creation:

> You are hostile towards me as you are towards all that you have not created.
>
> You only accept what comes from yourself. You only take what your own hands offer.
>
> You love *the other*, not for himself, but against me.

Thus the jealousy of the "other" turns out to be the writer's resentment of the fact that he cannot impose himself totally on the word, that the word transforms him while he tries to express *himself*. Expressing oneself becomes as impossible as knowing oneself. The blurring of the creator and the created (both are "I") is only the first step. The curious part is that the "other I" is created by the mirror of the word. The author (at least part of him) is created by the word. And yet, he says, *I* am at the origin of *their* existence.

In the exaltation of insight into his double self the writer imagines he has killed Yaël. A fusion of the two selves would indeed eliminate the word, our mental mirror. (In the chapter "The Three-paneled Mirror" the fusion of life and death destroys the mirror.) But there cannot possibly be such a fusion: we would cease to be human with the loss of our double, of our self-consciousness.

Two pages later, the narrator would strangle Yaël. Not just because she cannot be true (the word implies the possibility of ambiguity and lies), not just because he rages against the "other" as a false self, not even because his fusion with the "other" makes the mirror superfluous, but because the torment of the doubling is unbearable:

> I was no longer *the other*. He stood behind me. I realized that the immense distance Yaël had tried to put between us canceled the apparent distance between *the other* and me, so that I was the nightmare she fought by clutching her lover across my hands which did not let go of her neck.

The fusion was illusory. But what is more interesting is the comment on the respective distances between the protagonists. Only with the mirror at a distance, in an unreflected state, could the distance between the two selves be abolished, could man be at one with himself. But once you have looked into the mirror this is impossible. So man's task becomes "to be oneself in *the other*," in the reflection that the word creates of him in the book. And perhaps he succeeds all too well in this ambiguous task. Perhaps the writer is altogether transformed into his book, dies into the other?

> . . . you said to me: "Is this you?" Entering into your game I replied: "No." Then you threw yourself screaming into the arms of *the other:* "He's changing. He's forced to change too. It's not him. It's you."

The other will die with the author and the word in the book which is the only place where the word can die:

> You will die in the book where I am dying
> with *the other*, after God.

God, being a reflection of man, dies first as the light goes down on the mirror. But this death in the book is a death awaiting resurrection by a reader whose eye will create a new virtual space in which the game of reflection can continue with the reader taking part. For he will look for himself while acting as a mirror for the author's mirror-image in the book.

There is also a literal mirror in the book, a mirror with three panels. Yaël is about to give birth. "In the first mirror she smiles," thinking about her child. The doubling of the mirror is set in parallel to the doubling of procreation. The second mirror is split by Yaël's scream (or an object she hurls to attract attention) at the moment of parturition. The child is still-born. Hence "in the third mirror, the void engulfs the room." This sequence is commented thus:

> In the first mirror, O woman, the lie relished its spite.
> In the second mirror, O woman, the lie blew up.
> In the third mirror, O woman, truth questions itself.

It is the truth of death and the void which questions itself in the mirror faced with the panel in which the lie of life is smiling. It is the treachery of mirrors to contain both the earthly paradise and death. But their fusion in the birth of death, in the birth of the stillborn child, shatters the mirror.

It shatters the mirror because the game of reflection depends on alternation, on "the alternating of All and Nothing which appearance tries to mask" It cannot be resolved without going straight to the void. Appearance, the game of reflections, alternating between all and nothing is, of course, lies: "the lie of images. Mirror of a mirror, the universe lives by reflections." Edmond Jabès's mirrors say: all mirrors are lying. Edmond Jabès's words say: all words are lying. But this lie, or rather this oscillation between lie and truth that these paradoxes create, is the condition of life, of existence:

> Beings and things exist only in the mirrors which copy them. We are countless crystal facets where the world is reflected and drives us back to our own reflections, so that we can know ourselves only through the universe and what little it retains of us.

This new double mirror where the world is reflected in us and we in the world again recalls the end of *Return to the Book*: "Man does not exist. God does not exist. The world alone exists through God and man in the open book." The world exists, but only in the book, only through us and the mirrors we have created with their endless back and forth, perhaps only through the terror we feel at midpoint between the reflections and which is perhaps the locus of creation.

•

I ask Edmond if he feels close to Borges, to "Circular Ruins" in particular.

He would rather single out "Pierre Ménard, Author of Don Quixote." He seems to have some reservations and glances off into the biographical. He had looked forward to meeting Borges in Italy, in 1986, the very summer Borges died, he tells me. He is very moved by the story that Borges, if he likes a book read to him, wants to hold it in his hand, to caress certain pages with his fingers. As if he wanted to touch the "white fire" he cannot see.

•

> It is assumed here . . . that no human being is free from the strain of relating inner and outer reality, and that relief from this strain is provided by an intermediate area of experience which is not challenged (arts, religion, etc.). This intermediate area is in direct continuity with the play area of the child who is "lost" in play.
>
> *(D. W. Winnicott)*

Art can be this bridge between inner and outer world. Not just because it has license not to distinguish between true and false, subjective and objective. The work itself partakes of both realities. It is not pure form, pure potentiality. Its physical and mental dimensions—in the case of poetry, sound and meaning—are equally important. Poetry reminds us that words have bodies, that language is, in part, part of the physical world.

And while the page with its blank spaces stresses separation, sound connects. Sound has no borders.

"The Spirit is the Conscious Ear" (Emily Dickinson).

•

Jean Daive sits in front of La Chope, on the Place de la Contrescarpe, and sees Edmond Jabès walking in the distance:

> He regularly makes his rounds in the neighborhood, for hours. He walks in circles that first get larger and larger and then smaller and smaller. Hands crossed in back. His circles have two centers: the Place de la Contrescarpe and the building in rue de l'Epée de Bois where he lives.

•

In San Diego, in March 1983, I walk along the beach. Enormous bright walls are moving toward me. They are nothing like what I am used to calling "waves." My heart tries to adjust to their beat. As if my organs found their place inside this body of water. Overhead, strange triangular airplanes. Military. A science fiction feel.

When I arrive on campus for the afternoon seminar, Edmond and Arlette, to my surprise, are just returning from a drive to Mexico!

The University of California requires a Social Security number in order to pay any honorarium. Edmond Jabès has no such number. A foreigner can obtain one only outside the U.S. So Michael Davidson has driven him to Mexico, to the consulate in Tijuana.

"This is a chance to see the Californian desert," Michael had promised.

Edmond is not impressed:

"This is no desert. There are *flowers!*"

He seems a bit tired. First, a blank in the middle of an improvised speech. Then explicitly:

"We're doing publicity for Wesleyan."

"We can stop anytime."

"No, I've agreed."

"We can still cancel."

"No."

Rolling stone. Polished smooth by the desert sand. Sandy, grainy language. With an edge. Like the almost square pebbles from Brittany.

•

Michel de Certeau has asked Edmond Jabès to come to the Alliance Française in San Diego and answer questions. A group of friendly people want to meet the famous poet, but have not bothered to look at his books. There are no questions. I look at Michel de Certeau. He sits back, makes no move to get things going. Disaster, I think. But Edmond is not daunted. He begins telling a few Jewish jokes. He dwells on the one Keith remembers as Edmond's favorite:

A Jew from one village is bragging to a Jew from the next village. "Our rabbi," he says, "is the most learned, the most pious rabbi in the whole country. There is no rabbi to compare with ours.

> Why, our rabbi is so pious and *so* great, that every night Elijah comes down from heaven, into his very room, to consult with him."
>
> At this, the second Jew is outraged.
>
> "What? What's this you say? Elijah comes down? *Elijah* comes down from heaven to *your rabbi*?—Who told you that?"
>
> "I know it for a fact," the first Jew says. "Our rabbi told me himself."
>
> "Your rabbi told you? Your rabbi! You know what I think? I think your rabbi is a liar!"
>
> The first Jew would be offended at this, if it were not such patent nonsense.
>
> "Listen," he says. "How can you say our rabbi is a liar? You think, you *really think*, our rabbi could possibly be a liar! Well now, really, would Elijah come down *every night* to talk *to a liar*?"

From this circular logic, Edmond Jabès moves on with great ease to talk about the involutions in *The Book of Questions*.

•

A few days later, San Francisco. We stay with Michael Palmer and Cathy Simon. Undaunted by the no-salt imperative, Cathy cooks a wonderful lemon-stuffed chicken.

The reading at Fort Mason, on March 13, 1983, is my favorite of all: it not only has our usual alternation between French and English, but Jerome Rothenberg and I alternate the English. A double dialogue of voices and languages that seems to come from the heart of the work.

Beforehand, I notice George and Mary Oppen in the hall and take Edmond and Arlette to meet them. While Edmond and George talk, Mary thanks me because, she says, George gets tired very quickly now. They will not likely stay for the whole reading. Indeed I do not see them at the intermission.

John Taggart has dramatized this as Oppen "walking out" on Edmond Jabès, to the point of locating "*the* moment" when it must have occurred. I have my doubts. But it led him into curious if not very convincing speculations about Oppen's relation to his Jewish identity.

The next day, a group of us eat at Chez Panisse. Our young waiter excitedly tells Edmond that he was at the reading and loved it very much. Then comes back and presents Edmond with a bottle of wine. Edmond is visibly moved. He comes back to it several times. Always with the comment: this could not happen in France. And though he is not allowed any wine, the rest of us drink it very happily.

•

Back in Providence, we see *Little Red Riding Shawl* by John Emigh. It is a performance, in traditional Balinese style, of Little Red Riding Hood. John Emigh plays all the parts, including two narrators, one naive, the other with a jaundiced eye. It is the latter who finally concludes that "innocence is more agreeable than useful." Both Edmond and Arlette are delighted. There is much double entendre and slang. Whenever I whisper an explanation to Edmond, e.g., that the "rocks" that are made so much of also mean "balls," he whispers back: "Tell Arlette."

•

How fragile, how shortlived translation is. I have been quoting this passage:

> *Nous n'écrivons que ce qu'il nous a été accordé de lire et qui est une infime partie de l'univers à dire. Jamais le livre, dans son actualité, ne se livre.*
> We can only write what we have been given to read. It is an infinitesimal part of the universe to be told. The book in its actual state never surrenders.

I have claimed that this "livre" refers to the metaphorical book of the universe, of infinite potential, the Name of God that contains all language, the "book" that all writing "reads" and "translates." Hence *dans son actualité* is crucial, is the actual state of this book—the "actual" state of potential. This is an amazing statement. I still am not sure I understand it. Is it that potential does not surrender to actualization? To its actualization in the book? If we allow the pun on *livre* its play: it does not "book" itself? Or is it sheer paradox: the "actuality" of potentiality? Or is this the one unquestioned certainty of *The Book of Questions*: infinite potential exists? In which case this affirmation of possibility is so much taken for granted that it appears in a subordinate clause.

I look at my translation: "The book never actually surrenders." This now seems inadequate. The adverbial form weakens the statement, makes us read over it rather than pause to ponder its strangeness and implications. In 1973, I did not see this sentence as I see it today. This pleases me in as far as it shows my reading and interpretation are not frozen. But it is also demonstrates that there is no such thing as a "definitive" translation, even of one's own.

Not to mention that translations age in a way original texts do not. The "period" traits of my writing are unnoticeable to me and my contemporaries. In another century (assuming the books still exist) these traits will become visible, an obstacle to reading the "real" Jabès text, a spur to new translations. Whereas the period traits of Jabès are Jabès.

Translation: troubled transparency, clarity of imposture. Not likeness. The same and not the same. A rose is a rose. Is not.

> All translators live off the difference between languages, all translation is based on this difference, even while seeming to pursue the perverse aim to abolish it. *(Maurice Blanchot)*

•

Marcel Cohen, in "Quatre Anamnèses," recalls Edmond telling how he and Michel Leiris stood in front of a restaurant after lunch, still talking. Suddenly it starts to rain. "Should we not take shelter?" he asks, turning up his collar. "Yes of course," Leiris answers without however stopping. Since Leiris could hardly be unaware of the heavier and heavier drops hitting his bald head Edmond does not want to interrupt him a second time. So there they stand in the downpour, chatting, while all around them people are running for the next doorway.

•

Rue de l'Epée de Bois, even in the rain. There are lights on in the apartment on the second floor. There are no lights. The windows are closed. The balcony window is open, and an end of curtain blows out. The street is empty.

It is I who call it empty. I who am alive.

If I close my eyes, I see Edmond in Providence. He naps on the couch. The zigzags of the Navajo blanket push at the edges of his sleep. A sleep he returns from. Can still return from.

•

Once we visit Arlette when she is in the hospital for minor surgery and find Edmond and Claude there as well as enormous quantities of flowers. The other patient in the room objects to them, so Edmond has to take them home. After which Claude, Edmond, and we decide to eat together.

Keith remembers:

> Edmond, without Arlette to check his intake of salt, opted for Italian. Halfway through the meal, I began to feel ill. I tried not to succumb, but when it seemed serious, I announced that I had to leave and managed to get as far as the sidewalk where I passed out. Claude, having followed me out, caught me and told Rosmarie to quick call Police-Secours.
>
> I dreamt that I was throwing up and, like Adam's dream, woke and found it real. Rosmarie, meanwhile, about to call for help, realized the first question would be, Where are you? and realized also that she did not know. She came out to ask where we were and saw

that I had recovered enough that a taxi home would be the best program.

Arlette called, from the hospital, to see how I was.

I was desperately afflicted with the epizooties, an unimportant twenty-four-hour horror.

Recovering, I gave it to Rosmarie, who had a much worse case, but who—falling ill at home, not on the street—got less attention.

Edmond, from all the flowers he was saddled with, had an attack of asthma.

•

Edmond lifts his glass of wine. I know it is a dream, or it would have been water. He says: "Reb Wolgamot declared: 'As the shad roils its world of water, so memory stirs up shadows.' But Reb Alphery replied: 'Even when thirsty, avoid polluted water. You will know it by its troubled transparency. It has all the clarity of imposture. The imposture of the rabbi with the non-Sephardic name.' "

I recognize lines from *Désir d'un commencement Angoisse d'une seule fin*, that I have just been struggling to translate. But Reb Wolgamot goes farther back. I smuggled him into the first *Book of Questions*. Part of the covenant of the John Barton Wolgamot Society is that we try to put his name into all our books. I do not know if Edmond noticed it, if he read through the English after the book was printed. I don't think we ever read this passage in one of our bilingual readings.

But when Reb Av who discusses *l'avenir* metamorphosed into Reb Fu who discusses the future, Edmond asked:

"How did this Chinese rabbi get into my book?!"

It is true, all his rabbis have Sephardic names, so not only Fu, but Wolgamot sticks out—at best Ashkenase, but certainly close to my mother's maiden name.

•

Edmond's daughter Nimet, a nuclear physicist, comes to visit us in Providence. She shows us slides of "Nimet bumps," the nuclear phenomenon named after her. She also tells us that she has never read her father's books. But once when she was hospitalized, Edmond came to see her every day and told her his books.

Il m'a raconté ses livres.

•

Joseph Guglielmi's paralyzed son Raoul has let himself die. I see again Thérèse, his mother, who could not live with his accident and threw herself into the Seine. In my head, she is dancing the tango at Mitsou Ronat's party. Mitsou who is also dead. And Edmond and Arlette.

•

The body refuses to breathe, pushes at the door of night, of nothingness. The asthma gets worse as Edmond approaches the end of a book. Once finished, the book will reject him, will kick him out of the world he created. The writer is nobody, he says with his last breath, and nowhere. No body, no where, no breath, wind, spirit, inspiration. In the Book of Torment.

How distant it seems, the time when he could say "here" and "now." Here, on this page, now, these words, these voices.

•

In their essay on "Folklore as a Specific Form of Creation," Jakobson and Bogatyrev oppose folklore and literature in terms of *langue* and *parole*:

> From the point of view of the reciter, the traditional text represents a *fact of language* which is impersonal and has a life independent from the bard even though he can deform it and introduce new elements. . . . But for the literary author, the work represents a fact of *parole*. It is not a matter of a pre-existing donnée given to him a priori, but of something that has to be created by the individual. . . . The author of a literary work finds himself in the paradoxical situation of having to put forward a *parole* whose *langue* is absent or unknown.

My first reaction is: how deeply this resonates with Jabès's work. *Parole sans langue*. Utterance without code. The writer without place. People without land. No givens. No origins. Neither God nor country nor language.

But I immediately have doubts. There *never* is a preexisting *langue*. As I said earlier, the code presupposes utterance as much as the utterance presupposes the code. We all fabricate the language we speak and write. The "traditional text," too, comes about through the performances. Once it has been fixed to the point Jakobson describes, where it is simply "performed," it is dead. And the "traditional text," the "fact of language," has its counterpart for the author in the tradition of his genre. We don't create ex nihilo.

Jabès is subtler than such binary opposition. His *langue*, the "book," is both created by the writer *and* preexists. It is both read by the writer *and* is unavailable, absent, unknown. I quote once more:

> *Jamais le livre, dans son actualité, ne se livre.*
>
> What, then is this initial word? Maybe an unbearable absence of the word which the word will, unbeknownst to us, come to fill by exposing itself.

For translation, though, the distinction applies. The original is *a fact of language*, which has a life independent from the translation.

•

What can a writer do whose subject matter is the impossible, the emptiness of transcendence, the unsayable? He must join the nothingness. He must become invisible. Unseen in order to see.

Edmond Jabès writes a text over which he claims no authorial power, a text which he claims only to copy, make legible. This is a remarkable claim in itself. Postmodern theorists have echoed it in many variants while blithely continuing to speak authoritatively. But with Jabès it is not just the statement: everything in his work—the shifting voices and perspectives, the breaks of mode, tautologies, alogical sequences and contradictory metaphors, the stress on uncertainty (the constant subjunctive)—all combine to subvert the authority we expect in a book. Authority of statement, of closure and linearity, the confidence in a narrative thread, continuity of temporal and causal sequence. And most of all, the authority of the author.

> I don't presume to have any answers; I ask questions. If I give a special status to the question, that is because I find something unsatisfactory about the nature of the answer. . . . [A]nswers embody a certain form of power. Whereas the question is a form of non-power. But a subversive kind of non-power, one that will be upsetting to power.

•

What forms in the mind when we read a metaphor or comparison is a *third* element that arises in the gap between the two elements of the metaphor and goes beyond both. Thus it is the very opposite of binary thinking.

Jabès strips away his early Surrealist imagery for a sparser kind of writing. He undermines metaphor, but certainly does not return to the binary. He does not accept that a door has to be either open or closed, but, on the contrary, seems to isolate and enlarge this third element to the point where it both embodies the gap and fills it. His "pure gesture" of metaphor detaches the connecting function from the particular examples and thus opens a vista on the functioning of the mind—thus rejoining the Surrealists in one of their intentions, across the stylistic differences. And he reinforces this third element by the white spaces which, while separating blocks of text, connect them in the space of the page and set them in a relation that brings home the lack of transition.

Questioning the image still acknowledges its power.

•

"I have little taste for images" the *Nouvel Observateur* headlined Jabès's text on Degottex. In the text, the statement is much less categorical:

> My landscape is the desert. I grew up with this landscape—but is it a landscape?—before losing myself in it. There are no colors in the desert. There is the infinite of color.
>
> In the desert, color does not hold the eye, does not stop it. It lets the eye go through it. Transparency. Nudity. This accounts perhaps for my having little taste for images; but it's more complicated than that.

It is indeed more complicated than that. Jean Frémon titles his introduction to Jabès's writings on art: "Against the Image?"—with a very important question mark. He sees the taboo on representation behind Jabès's conflictual relation to the image, but also wonders, not altogether convincingly, if another factor might not be that the first artistic forms Jabès encountered were the frescos and bas-reliefs of Upper Egypt, the most sublime—and abstract—art ever. In any case, he notes a greater intensity, a reaction almost of terror, when Jabès writes on figurative artists like Bacon or Saura. Which makes him say: "the representation of the face is the true question."

The face. Not color. As with the "infinite of color" in the desert, we have seen that the painter's overload of color and the writer's excess of metaphor can exorcise itself and lead to transparency.

Transparency. Light. Is this why he has such a taste for movies, even TV? If the TV is on, Edmond admits, he cannot tear himself away from watching, even if it is the trashiest show. Images are irresistible to him. Their force is overwhelming. It's a good thing, he laughs, that he doesn't have a TV here, in rue de l'Epée de Bois.

•

In 1983/84 Keith and I live off the Place de la Bastille. That year we are well informed on all demonstrations because they either begin or end there. But no matter what political persuasion, all banners proclaim for LA LIBERTE and against L'INFAMIE.

That year, we develop a Sunday ritual with Edmond and Arlette: afternoon movie followed by dinner. I remember best the ones that prompt Edmond into parodies. He mimics to perfection the melodramatic, macho way Vittorio Gassman sets his shoulders in *Benvenuta*.

•

Edmond is convinced that science is a kind of poetry. Discoveries require imagination—in the literal sense, images. It was, for instance, Kekulé's dream of two serpents biting their tails that helped him find the molecular structure of benzene.

Images as the basis of thought. To see is to know. Etymology says so: we postulate an Indo-European root, *weid,* to see, as the basis of "wisdom," "wit," intelligence, knowledge.

Now, the neurologists have come to the same conclusion: There is a structural similarity between the patterns of brain activity and the shape of the external stimulus. And this ability to form images ("body-representing neural structures"), to order and recall them, is what Antonio R. Damasio sees as constituting the mind:

> It is often said that thought is made of much more than images . . . words and non-image abstract symbols. . . . [But] both words and arbitrary symbols are based on topographically organized representations and can become images. Most of the words we use in our inner speech exist as auditory or visual images in our consciousness. If they did not become images, however fleetingly, they would not be anything we could know.

"The body-minded brain," says Damasio. Poetry: the body-minded language. The body of the word has its reasons that our reason must follow.

•

Rue Auguste Comte. The wet pavement reflects the street lamps, but no trees even though I am between the Luxembourg and Observatoire gardens. Was it here, perhaps on our way to a movie at the Lucernaire Forum, that Edmond said the streets of Paris try to approach the mineral splendor of desert?

•

Barbara Einzig writes of Edmond Jabès:

> Your eyes lived among your face, as if it too were a wilderness. . . . You were able to keep your own company in silence, and so we leaned forward when you spoke. You kept silent as you spoke, and the time in which you spoke was not the time that we inhabited. Yet it occurred there, and because of this I thought of you as a magician.

•

In the fall of 1983, a new center for Jewish studies, the Centre Rachi, is being inaugurated in Paris. Edmond Jabès is to give a reading. At the door, we are frisked. I know there have been a number of anti-Jewish manifestations recently, a bomb in Goldberg's restaurant, swastikas in the cemeteries, but I am still a bit taken aback. It turns out the Israeli ambassador is here and will speak first. With Israeli-Palestinian relations what they are the high security makes sense.

I recognize many faces in the auditorium. On the podium, Edmond Jabès, the director of the Centre, the ambassador, and another person.

The ambassador begins by referring to the Palestinians as "those assassins"—and immediately some people in the audience start to walk out.

A few more hawkish sentences, and Arlette Jabès, in the first row, gets up and leaves, followed by many others, Claude Royet-Journoud among them. Keith and I hesitate. We decide to take our cue from Edmond.

The ambassador invokes the Masada, Judas Maccabeus, "the hammer," and again "those assassins, those criminals, those new Nazis." He calls for a Holy War.

Edmond gets up, gathers his papers, and leaves the podium.

No point in staying after this.

The hall outside the auditorium is packed. The security guards make it into a pandemonium. They rush from group to group, in a tizzy, trying to get people either back into the auditorium or out the door.

Nobody budges.

We make our way to where Edmond and Arlette are standing.

"Are you still going to read?"

"Let's wait and see."

Then six bodyguards hurry the scowling ambassador through the crowd to the exit.

We move back into the hall. Edmond reads. Wonderfully. And to a standing ovation.

Afterward, he tells us:

"As I started to get up, the director next to me grabbed hold of my trousers, trying to keep me there. So my great fear was that I would lose my pants up there on the podium."

During the following days, Jabès gets many telegrams, calls, letters from Israel:

"How could you do this, how could you walk out on the ambassador?"

But, while being deeply concerned with Israel and its fate, Edmond Jabès has always distinguished between the dream of a Jewish land and the actual State of Israel, which he does not consider above criticism.

•

We play Carissimi for Edmond and Arlette. "Jephtha's daughter." *Fugite cedite fugite cedite, impii.* The horns of victory. Then the heartrending lament. Penetrating. That she died a virgin. Unpenetrated.

•

Keith remembers how once, when the Jabèses are in Providence, a colleague of his comes by in a great flurry and in his jogging suit. He is supposed to introduce John Hollander tonight and he has never read a word of Hollander's. We lend him some books.

We go, with Edmond and Arlette, to the reading, and Edmond's eyes widen to hear the colleague tell how much, over so many years, he has enjoyed the poetry of John Hollander.

Afterwards, Edmond acts out jogging through those many years.

The joggers we encounter on our walks in Providence puzzle Edmond.

"First they get in their cars and drive for miles. Then they get out and run like mad. Then they get back in their cars and drive for miles."

He acknowledges their appearance with: *encore un fou*. Another madman.

•

After each volume, Edmond is afraid I will stop translating. Each time I continue he is relieved. He pretends not to pressure me. He tells me he understands the claims of jobs, and of my own writing. But he manages to drop little hints:

"You know I won't be around forever to answer your questions."

Till we're both laughing. Another time, he is astonished that I am translating some German poems: "You must not tire yourself out!"

He especially keeps at me to translate the poem *Récit*. Not that I would not like to, but here is the first line: *Il et son feminin île,* "He and his feminine form," and: "he and his feminine island"—from which he is *ex-ilé*.

The whole poem is built on this pun. "He" is incomplete without his feminine, he is the restless sea washing around the island. I try to think of solutions. Can I work with "exile" and "isle"? No, it seems forced. Whereas, for all its being invented, the formation of the feminine *ile* is so within French linguistic habits that I almost wonder it doesn't exist.

I try to explain that the puns in his prose work have space around them for approximation and experiment, but the pun in this poem does not.

"Why don't you leave the pun in French, as you often did in *El, ou le dernier livre*?"

"That was different. No one of those puns was central to the book. Whereas here, the whole poem depends on it."

I still have not translated it. I am still thinking about it. It is this kind of word-play that fascinates me. Word-work so deeply imbedded in the language that it seems to show its chemistry at work. Here the formation of a feminine from the masculine by the added letter *e*. It is almost Eve created from Adam's rib, with this extra bone Adam no longer has.

•

As soon as the temperature drops below 50°F. it is *un froid de canard* for Edmond and Arlette. When he is invited to Montréal, Arlette is sure they are going to freeze. She buys heavy plastic "moon boots," the kind the astronauts wear. She is disappointed that she does not get to wear them. She is never long enough outside, and they are much too warm indoors. On the way back she leaves them with me. They are definitely too warm for Paris. I wear them the few times we get a snow storm in Providence. But I see Arlette walking across vast snowy fields on the moon, in slow motion.

•

To continue. To carry from one place to another. To continue thinking, to think from another place, another perspective. The content of memory changes as I approach it from a different place, myself a different person.

Between Cairo and Paris, between *Je bâtis ma demeure* and *Le livre des questions*, falls the experience of being a Jew in a hostile society. *As experience*, not as imaginative and intellectual empathy. What he had known abstractly, he now knows in his body. Expulsion from Egypt for the most arbitrary of reasons: race. There are themes that a writer is not free to choose, themes that impose themselves in the manner of an illness or a wound.

> Mark the first page of the book with a red marker. For, in the beginning, the wound is invisible.

Edmond Jabès describes the change in his writing as giving up the Oriental and the visible:

> My first images were images of the Orient, and my landscape an Oriental landscape. But I did not stay on this side of the visible. Too seductive, too captivating, Oriental poetry is like a fresco. I am also interested in the back of the fresco, in the back of the wall.

As Daniel Lançon points out, Jabès's Egyptian poems tried desperately to be part of French poetry, whereas "*The Book of Questions* places Edmond Jabès on the margin of the Western poetic tradition he had dreamed of entering."

But I have to disagree when he continues:

> It is in some way a "return to the Orient" we are watching, as if underneath the European and modern interrogation of the book, the sign, the problematic of writing, the personal destiny of a poet after all Oriental . . . claimed its place.

Rather than a "return to the Orient," this work is, in fact, an extraordinary gift of Oriental rhythms and forms that Jabès brings to his adopted culture. So that Jabès achieved in exile, and on a very different level, what his early efforts for Franco-Egyptian friendship could not. Rather than bringing French traditions into Egypt, he has brought Oriental traditions into France.

•

What can writing do?

Ask questions.

Klagen und anklagen. Lament and accuse have the same root in German. Lament implies an accusation.

Make visible. Shed light.

On the first day of creation, light comes out of the word of the creator. It immediately introduces separation (as it cannot coexist with darkness) and time (in the alternation with the dark). It creates along with God. According to Kabbalistic tradition this pure spiritual light of the first day *was,* but did not remain. Where did it go? Into the Torah. That is, into the word.

In *The Book of Questions,* rabbis and guests always gather around the lamp. A lamp which is, of course, also the book. When I translate Jabès, my thesaurus is always open at "light," to cope with all the shades and degrees of luminosity invoked.

•

Raymond Federman asks why I have translated Edmond Jabès. I sense that he wants me to say: to atone. After all, I am German. Was. I was taught the Nazi salute along with the alphabet. But this is not it. *Ce n'est pas ça*, as Edmond would say. It would be presumptious to think that I, that any one individual *could.* Besides, I have not translated Elie Wiesel or any other holocaust literature. It is this particular work that touched me.

On the other hand, who knows what motives play into our actions. I do not know what pulls me to the place where I must, and want to, speak. Here. Where I am. "We always search for the meaning of our own life in the text we translate," says Dominique Grandmont. And sometimes we "find the other inside ourselves."

•

Edmond walks, slowly. Tired, perhaps, but more following the slow rhythms in his head. Walks and talks. Step by sentence and sentence by step. On and on. Hands crossed in back. Holding already the paragraph to come, not dispersing into the night.

•

I look at photos. His dashing Rudolf Valentino look from the thirties. Snapshots of our travels. One shot "in drag."

When we are planning his first trip to the U.S., he says:

"What will happen when I go to New York? I will show you." He comes back as "Mrs. Finkelstein," in Arlette's coat and hat, pants rolled up to his knees. "Mrs. Finkelstein" tries to kidnap Edmond Jabès for a charitable bazaar, a recital by Jewish orphans, dinner with the rabbi, and especially the synagogue.

"Mister Jabès, you must go to the synagogue."

"I don't want to go to the synagogue."

"Oh, but you must . . ."

"I won't go to the synagogue."

"You, the son of a rabbi . . ."

"I will *not* go to the synagogue."

"And you a writer . . ."

"I tell you I won't."

"You must come and read the Book of the Book . . ."

"My Book of the Book is *The Book of Questions*."

More serious, the portraits. The one from 1972 on the Wesleyan books, by Bernard Carrère. In three-quarter profile, sticking out his chin—pace sculptor Kono—severe.

The sequence by David Harali which Edmond himself has called "parlant," where I indeed can almost hear him talk, struggle with a thought, search for words, brighten once he has found the formulation, the wrinkles smoothed out, momentarily.

But the portrait that haunts me is by Maxim Godard, taken three weeks before Edmond's death. He stands between the shutters of his balcony window. He looks at the camera, at me, out of deep furrows. Now his eyes seem more waiting than ready to come forward.

I prefer his pictures as an "old" man. They are the Edmond I knew. The marked face that could be nobody else's. The slack cheeks I can still feel against my lips.

The photos, like memory, play the possible against the real, play at reviving as possibility what has been. And only revive grief.

•

I hear the voices Edmond Jabès invented, that spoke through him. They accompany me. They have absorbed his voice, his voice wandering among them, have now absorbed it altogether.

Like and unlike death, which does not stop time but allows one of its dimensions to absorb the others. The dead man's present and future take the form of memory, the past.

But the books remain. They have absorbed him into their own continuous present.

•

A photograph of Michael Gizzi comes in the mail. He looks more and more like Edmond.

I see us in the car with Michael, in 1986. He has arranged for Edmond Jabès to read at Simon's Rock and is driving us across Massachusetts to the Berkshires. We are driving into the afternoon sun. Arlette and Michael talk about gardens: Arlette, about real ones she has been in; Michael, about the gardens in his book, *Species of Intoxication,* its "prefer'd exquisite flowering" and the

> giddy little manic soul flanked by buds, the endurin' sprinkle
> of blue

of the poem beginning "Cher Edmond Jabès." Their conversation precipitates Michael's sequence of poems, *Gyptian in Hortulus,* dedicated to Arlette Jabès.

•

I thought Arlette was the thread that tied Edmond to life. It seems it was the other way round. She survives him by a mere year and a half.

•

I haunt the places where he lived, the streets he walked—and he the poet of the non-place. Rue de l'Epée du Bois. The windows of the apartment are closed. I look at the roof silhouetted against the cloud that drifts to the right and spills, while more clouds from the left come and devour the sky, erase even the roofs, so low. As if they had to enact Edmond Jabès's words.

I say "I." I do not pretend to objectivity. Or even truth. *My*

Edmond Jabès? How absurd to say "mine." I cannot even claim that this is how he lives in my memory. No, this is less than his presence in my memory even though my memory is notoriously bad.

> There is no place not the reflection of another. It is the reflected place we must discover. The place within the place.
>
> I write at the mercy of this place.

The last summer we spend together, he works on a text for Maria Elena Vieira da Silva. He shows me reproductions of her work. He feels close to her. She too is building her cityscapes, her "suspended gardens" in a void, a non-place.

I see some kinship with the Angelopoulos behind Edmond's desk.

"No, that's not it. She paints as if in broken mirrors."

Now I read in *Un regard: "There was a place*. It is in this *'there was'* that she takes her place; in this absence to be explored."

Too many images that do not speak. Incongruous underbrush invading the stone of the city. The past invades, grows rank over the present. But I go on to do my errands. I buy cheese at Arlette's favorite crèmerie, buy bread and walk down the steps of métro Monge.

•

Once when Edmond and Arlette arrive in Providence, we are about to have our roof repaired. But we are not expecting the workmen for another week, so we do not mention it right away, on their arrival. The next morning, Arlette is awakened by a commotion. She opens the curtains, sees a ladder leaning against the house, and thinks "Fire!" Just then a man appears on the ladder, smiles and waves, "Hi."

Both Edmond and Arlette love recounting the story in the weeks to follow. Arlette, to exorcise, to laugh away her fright. Edmond, to embroider: both Arlette and the roofers had felt the spiritual fire of our encounter. It would act as a charm and prevent any actual fire.

Bavardage. Small talk. Like a warm bath relaxing his, our, anxiety. But Edmond Jabès's talk doesn't stay small for long.

Rosie Pinhas-Delpuech asks Edmond about the languages in his childhood:

Ma langue maternelle est une langue étrangère.—"My mother tongue is a foreign language."

•

A passionate questioning. Of himself, of human nature. Of what is considered a given. A passionate crying out against ignorance, willful blindness, against not understanding, not wanting to understand, against not communicating. A passionate questioning of language. Not just writing well, but staking his whole life on the word, on his call for a little light out of the overwhelming darkness.

Out of great need.

Out of our wounds.

•

I choose to sit in the café Danton that serves its sugar cubes wrapped in portraits of Rimbaud or Proust over the café that serves the history of the *gendarmerie*. Who wouldn't. When I saw Edmond Jabès for the last time, the sugar came wrapped in the French Revolution.

I heard Mei-mei Berssenbrugge say, "I have mourned my mother for one year. Now I will stop." Surprised at the precise time limit specified, I learned that this is Chinese tradition. Also, I suspect, wisdom. I myself have a messier sense of mourning, that it is perhaps never done altogether, that it is, like memory for Aristotle, a delayed motion that continues to exist in the soul.

NOTES

The works of Edmond Jabès and their translations are quoted with the following abbreviations (the publishers are Gallimard (Paris) and Wesleyan University Press [UP] (Middletown, Connecticut), respectively, unless otherwise indicated):

JBD	***Je bâtis ma demeure: poemes 1943–1957*** (1959)	———	[No English translation]
The Book of Questions:			
LQ	*Le Livre des Questions* (1963)	BQ	*The Book of Questions* (1976)
LY	*Le Livre de Yukel* (1964)	BYRB	*The Book of Yukel / Return to the Book* (1977)
RL	*Retour au Livre* (1965)		
Y	*Yaël* (1967)		
E	*Elya* (1969)		
A	*Aely* (1972)	YEA	*Yaël, Elya, Aely* (1983)
EL	*El, ou le dernier livre* (1973)	ELLB	*El, or the Last Book* (1984)
The Book of Resemblances:			
LR	*Le Livre des Ressemblances* (1976)	BR	*The Book of Resemblances* (1990)
LR2	*Le Soupçon le Désert* (1978)	BR2	*Intimations The Desert* (1991)
LR3	*L'ineffacable l'inaperçu* (1980)	BR3	*The Ineffaceable The Unperceived* (1992)
R	***Récit*** (Fata Morgana, 1981)	———	[No English translation]
The Book of Limits:			
PLS	*Le petit livre de la subversion hors de soupçon* (1982)	LBS	*The Little Book of Unsuspected Subversion* (Stanford UP, 1996)
LD	*Le Livre du Dialogue* (1984)	BD	*The Book of Dialogue* (1987)

P	*Le Parcours* (1985)	———	[No English translation]
LP	*Le Livre du Partage* (1987)	BS	*The Book of Shares* (Chicago UP, 1989)
LM	*Le Livre des Marges* (Fata Morgana, 1987)	BM	*The Book of Margins* (Chicago UP, 1993)
ET	*Un Etranger avec, sous le bras, un livre de petit format* (1989)	F	*A Foreigner Carrying in the Crook of His Arm a Tiny Book* (1993)
LH	*Le Livre de l'Hospitalité* (1991)	———	[No English translation]
UR	*Un regard* (Fata Morgana, 1992)	———	[No English translation]
DL	*Du Désert au livre: entretiens avec Marcel Cohen* (Belfond, 1980)	DB	*From the Desert to the Book: Dialogues with Marcel Cohen* (Station Hill, 1990)

The book incorporates material from my essays: "Edmond Jabès and the Impossible Circle," *Sub/Stance* 5/6 (winter/spring, 1973); "Mirrors and Paradoxes," *Kentucky Romance Quarterly* 26, no. 2 (1979), reprinted in *The Sin of the Book*, ed. Eric Gould (Lincoln: Univ. of Nebraska Press, 1985); "Silence, the Devil, and Jabès," in *The Art of Translation: Voices from the Field*, ed. Rosanna Warren (Boston: Northeastern Univ. Press, 1989); and "Le double miroir," trans. Pierre Lochak, in *Portrait(s) d'Edmond Jabès*, ed. Steven Jaron (Paris: Bibliothèque nationale de France, 1999).

p. 1: "The writer is nobody,": BQ 27.
"L'écrivain n'est personne," LQ 28.

p. 1: "Man does not exist,": BYRB 236.
L'homme n'existe pas. Dieu n'existe pas. Seul existe le monde à travers Dieu et l'homme dans le livre ouvert. RL 100.

p. 1: "You are the one who writes,": BQ 11.
"Tu es celui qui écrit et qui est écrit." LQ 9.

p. 2: "We know of silence,": F 45.
Nous ne connaissons, du silence, que ce que la parole peut nous en dire.

Que tu le veuilles ou non, c'est la parole seule que nous entérinons. ET 67.

p. 2: "Four graves,": BYRB 145.
Quatre tombes. Trois pays. La mort connaît-elle les frontières? Une famille. Deux continents. Quatre villes. Trois drapeaux. Une langue, celle du néant. Une douleur. RL 7.

p. 2: "Mark the first page,": BQ 13.
Marque d'un signet rouge la première page du livre, car la blessure est invisible à son commencement. LQ 11.

p. 3: "If we say 'I' ,": LH 35 (my translation).
". . . dire 'Je' c'est, déjà, dire la différence." LH 35.

p. 3: "And Serge Segal,": BQ 163.
Et Serge Segal, s'adressant aux prisonniers parqués autour de lui qui, bientôt, seront disséminés dans les divers camps d'extermination préparés à leur intention, comme s'il s'exprimait, au nom du Seigneur à Son peuple rassemblé, s'écria: "Vous êtes tous Juifs, même les antisémites, car vous avez été désignés pour le martyre. LQ 179/80.

p. 3: "Ah, the dead,": BY 31.
"Ah les morts sont tous juifs." "Qui est plus étranger qu'un homme défunt?" LY 33.

p. 3: "Rejected by your people,": BQ 61/2.
"Renié des tiens, volé de ton héritage, qui es-tu?" . . .
"Ne faire aucune différence entre un Juif et celui qui ne l'est pas, n'est-ce pas déjà ne plus être Juif?" . . .
Me frappant la poitrine avec mon poing, j'ai pensé:
"Je ne suis rien.
J'ai la tête tranchée.
Mais un homme ne vaut-il pas un homme?
Et le décapité le croyant?" LQ 64/5.

p. 4: "You are the one who writes,": BQ 11, LQ 9.

p. 4: "I talked to you,": BQ 122.
Je vous ai parlé de la difficulté d'être Juif, qui se confond avec la diffi-

culté d'écrire; car le judaïsme et l'écriture ne sont qu'une même attente, un même espoir, une même usure. LQ 132.

p. 4: "Defeat is,": BQ 19.
"La défaite est le prix consenti." LQ 17.

p. 5: "The Jew answers,": BQ 116.
"A toute question, le Juif répond par une question.
—Tu vois, dit Reb Mendel, au bout du raisonnement, il y a toujours, en suspens, une question décisive." LQ 125/6.

p. 6: "Privé d'R,": EL 39, ELLB 33.

p. 6: ". . . the aphorism,": Jabès, interview with Paul Auster, in *The Sin of the Book*, ed. Eric Gould (Lincoln: Univ. of Nebraska Press, 1985), p. 15. The interview was originally published in *Montemora* 6 (1979).

p. 6: "Who are you, Yukel?,": BQ 32/33.
Qui es-tu, Yukel?
Qui seras-tu?
"Tu", c'est quelquefois "Je".
Je dis "Je" et je ne suis pas "Je". "Je" c'est toi et tu vas mourir. Tu es vidé.
Désormais, je serai seul . . .
Et c'est moi qui te force à marcher; moi qui sème tes pas.
Et c'est moi qui pense, qui parle pour toi, qui cherche et qui cadence; car je suis écriture
et toi blessure.
T'ai-je trahi, Yukel?
Je t'ai sûrement trahi. LQ 34/35.

p. 7: "If translation has,": Haroldo de Campos, "Transluciferation," *Ex* 4 (1985), pp. 10–14 (my translation).

p. 7: "an inaccurate transmission,": Walter Benjamin, "The Task of the Translator," in *Illuminations,* trans. Harry Zohn (New York: Schocken, 1969), pp. 69–70.

p. 7: "blank spot on the map,": Emmanuel Hocquard, "Blank Spots," trans. Stacy Doris, *Boundary2* 26, no.1 (Spring 1999), p. 22; "Faire quelque chose avec ça," in *A Royaumont: traduction collective 1983–2000* (Grâne, France: Créaphis, 2000), pp. 401, 403. Cf. also *Les dernières nouvelles de la cabane* 18 (16 July 1999).

p. 7: "He is counting,": BQ 21.
"Il compte les pas qui le séparent de sa vie." LQ 21.

p. 7: "the kernel,": BQ 126.
"le noyau d'une rupture," LQ 137.

p. 8: "Through the ear,": ELLB 63.
"Nous nous introduirons, par l'ouïe, dans l'invisibilité des choses." EL 73.

p. 8: "To abandon oneself,": Nicolas Abraham, *Rhythms*, trans. Benjamin Thigpen and Nicholas T. Rand (Stanford, Calif.: Stanford Univ. Press, 1995), pp. 21, 23.

p. 9: "If writing is to remain,": Josh Cohen [University of London], "Infinite Desertion: Edmond Jabès, Maurice Blanchot and the Writing of Auschwitz," *forthcoming*. Joseph Kronick, *Derrida and the Future of Literature* (Albany: State Univ. of New York Press, 1999), p. 84.

p. 9: So when the artist: Robert Groborne, *Une lecture* . . . (Évreux, France: Æncrages & Co., 1976).

p. 9: "As for this distribution,": Jabès, interview with Paul Auster, *The Sin of the Book*, p. 15.

p. 9: "Yes, one can"; "One has to,": DB 62.
"Oui, on le peut. Et, même, on le doit. Il faut écrire à partir de cette cassure, de cette blessure sans cesse ravivée." DL 93.

p. 10: "the quality of silence,": Chris Chen, "The Afterlife of the Poem: an Appreciation of Paul Celan," *tripwire* 2 (fall 1998), p. 168.

p. 10: "That day,": BM 149
Ce jour-là. Le dernier. Paul Celan chez moi. Assis à cette place que mes yeux, en cet instant, fixent longuement.

Paroles, dans la proximité, échangées. Sa voix? Douce, la plupart du temps. Et cependant, ce n'est pas elle, aujourd'hui, que j'entends mais le silence. Ce n'est pas lui que je vois mais le vide, peut-être parce que, ce jour-là, nous avions l'un et l'autre, sans le savoir, fait le tour cruel de nous-mêmes. LM 157.

p. 11: "For me the words 'Jew,' ": DB 57.
"Le mot 'juif', le mot 'Dieu', c'est vrai, sont pour moi des métaphores: 'Dieu,' métaphore du vide; 'juif', tourment de Dieu, du vide." DL 87.

p. 11: "The very condition,": BM 191.
"La condition même de son incondition: *n'être pas*." LM 200.

p. 11: *dunamis*: Aristotle; see book Theta of *Metaphysics*, 1050b. 10, quoted by Giorgio Agamben, *Homo Sacer I: Le pouvoir souverain et la vie nue* (Paris: Editions du Seuil, 1997), pp. 54–55.

p. 11: "To write as if addressing God,": YEA 153.
Ecrire, comme si l'on s'adressait à Dieu; mais qu'attendre du néant où tout parole est désarmée? E 55.

p. 11: ". . . Truth is the void,": BQ 117.
—La vérité, c'est le vide, répondit Reb Mendel.
—Si la vérité qui est dans l'homme est le vide, reprit le plus ancien disciple, nous ne sommes que le néant dans un corps de chair et de peau. Dieu qui est notre vérité est donc aussi le néant?
—Dieu est une question, répondit Reb Mendel, une question qui nous conduit à Lui qui est Lumière par nous, pour nous qui ne sommes rien. LQ 126.

p. 12: "*Dieu = Vide = Vie d'yeux*,": ELLB 72.
Dieu = Vide = Vie d'yeux.

Il disait: "Dieu est vide du vide. Dieu est vie du vide. Il est vide d'une vie d'yeux. La mort est l'oeil du deuil."

Cieux, mot pluriel composé d'yeux et de ciel.

Dieu est également dans le mot Cieux, comme un unique silence—D, dans le miroir de la page, se transformant en C au premier frottement de la gomme.

Cieux, pluriel silencieux de Dieu.

Dieu. Di eu. Dis (à) eux. Vide entre deux syllabes. Dieu nous donne à dire le deuil.

Tu écriras indifféremment Dieux pour Dieu et Lieux pour Lieu; car Dieu est Dieux en Dieu et Lieux en Lieu.

Tout deuil est d'abord deuil de Dieu. EL 84.

Cf. also Felix Philipp Ingold, ". . . schreiben heisst geschrieben werden . . . ," in *Und Jabès* (Stuttgart: Legueil, 1994), pp. 125–53.

p. 13: "Do you know,": YEA 203.
"Sais-tu, dit-il, que le point final du livre est un oeil et qu'il est sans paupières?"
Dieu, il écrivait *D'yeux.* "D pour désir, ajoutait-il. Désir de voir. Désir d'être vu."
Trait pour trait, Dieu resemble à son Nom et son Nom est la Loi." A 7.

p. 13: "The name of God,": DB 102.
"Le nom de Dieu est la juxtaposition de tous les mots de la langue. Chaque mot n'est qu'un fragment détaché de ce nom." DL 142.

p. 13: "traveling inside the word,": see Marc-Alain Ouaknin, *Concerto pour quatre consonnes sans voyelles,* 2nd ed. (Paris: Payot & Rivages, 1998), pp. 75 ff.

p. 13: "permits a rediscovery,": DB 95 (Joris's translation mistakenly puts "rereading of the *book*").
". . . permet une redécouverte, une relecture du mot. On ouvre un mot comme on ouvre un livre: c'est le même geste." DL 134

p. 13: "The imperious mobilisation,": Joseph Guglielmi, *La Ressemblance impossible: Edmond Jabès* (Paris: Les Editeurs Français Réunis, 1978), p. 41 (my translation). Elsewhere, he sees it as a literalism that frees words from their discursive function: "Seul compte le travail *littéral* qui arrache la parole, le verbe . . . à leur enracinement séculaire, les jette sur les voies ignorées de l'exil et du désert"; p. 23.

p. 13: God, who is the point: cf. "God refused image and language in order to be Himself the point." ELLB 15.
"Dieu refusa l'image, refusa la langue afin d'être Soi-même le point." EL 19.

p. 13: "In Hebrew,": DB 82.
En hébreu, le point est la voyelle. Il permet au mot d'être lu, entendu. Si le point vient à manquer, il y a risque de contre-sens grossier. En fait, il n'y a pas de mot. Il y a des consonnes en attente de devenir vocable.
L'absence de points, dans les grands textes juifs traditionnels, continue de requérir une attention particulière du lecteur qui doit, de lui-même, recréer le mot, ce qui implique, plus qu'une profonde compréhension du texte, une véritable intuition de celui-ci. C'est à ce stade que le lecteur rejoint le créateur . . . DL 118. Cf. also Ouaknin, *Concerto*, p. 14.

p. 14: "The sex is always a vowel,": quoted in Gabriel Bounoure, *Edmond Jabès: la demeure et le livre* (Montpellier, France: Fata Morgana, 1984), p. 88: "Le sexe est toujours une voyelle." In his introduction to *Je bâtis ma demeure*, Bounoure goes as far as specifying the sex of the vowel as female: "To the consonants that outline the masculine structure of the word are married the changing nuances, the fine and nuanced colorations of the feminine vowels." *Je bâtis ma demeure*, p. 16.

p. 14: "a rape,": DB 102.
"Lire les mots derrière les mots—le déchiffrement du livre est infini—ne peut s'opérer que par un viol. C'est, d'une certaine manière, violer le Nom intouchable de Dieu." DL 142.

p. 14: "The liberties taken,": DB 94.
Une telle liberté prise à leur égard ouvre un abîme: celui des infinies possibilités offertes par le maniement des lettres et dont nous ne pourrons jamais revendiquer que l'arbitraire assemblage. C'est pourquoi le mot nous échappera toujours. DL 133.

p. 14: "A slightly larger space,": ELLB 17.
Un espace un peu plus large—la séparation de deux syllabes, par exemple—dans le mot, une faille inattendue, la cassure d'une lettre ou sa chute dans le vide, provoquent un tel jeu dans ce mot que celui-ci se voit entraîner dans une série de métamorphoses qui l'annule à mesure qu'elle progresse. EL 21.

p. 14: "If God is,": BQ 31.
Si Dieu est, c'est parce qu'Il est dans le livre; si les sages, les saints et les prophètes existent, si les savants et les poètes, si l'homme et l'insecte

existent, c'est parce qu'on trouve leurs noms dans le livre. Le monde existe parce que le livre existe; car exister, c'est croître avec son nom. LQ 32/3.

p. 15: "I took you in as a word,": YEA 12.
"Je te reçus, telle une parole." Y 20.

p. 15: "We become the word,": DB 90.
"Nous devenons le mot qui donne réalité à la chose, à l'être." DL 128.

p. 15: "absurd and fertile quest,": BQ 39.
"La vérité est, ainsi, dans le temps, cette absurde et fertile quête du mensonge . . ." LQ 41.

p. 15: to stay on the surface: cf. BQ 54, LQ 55.

p. 15: "has been given,": YEA 13.
". . . savoir si la parole ne nous a été donné que pour que nous puissions nous installer confortablement dans le mensonge?" Y 20.

p. 15: "potential space,": D. W. Winnicott, *Playing and Reality* (New York: Tavistock, 1989), p. 100.

p. 15: "I will tell you,": BQ 87.
"Je vous parlerai du prix qu'il a payé pour mentir, c'est-à-dire pour vivre." LQ 94.

p. 16: *"Jamais le livre,"*: E 50. "The book never actually surrenders." YEA 150.

p. 16: "The book carries all,": Jabès, interview with Auster, *The Sin of the Book*, p. 22. Cf. also DB 82, DL 118.

p. 16: "What book,": BYRB 123.
"—De quel livre parles-tu?
—Je parle du livre qui est dans le livre.
—Y a-t-il un livre caché dans celui que je lis?
—Il y a le livre que tu écris." BY 129.

p. 16: "The invisible form,": BYRB 231.
"L'invisible forme du livre est le corps lisible de Dieu." RL 95.

p. 16: neither is a key: Stéphane Mosès, "Son nom de cristal," *Instants* 1: *Pour Edmond Jabès* (1989), p. 20.

p. 16: in opposition to writing: cf. Jacques Derrida, *De la grammatologie* (Paris: Editions de Minuit, 1967), pp. 30–31.

p. 17: "Writing a book,": YEA 36.
Ecrire le livre c'est associer sa voix à celle, virtuelle, des marges, c'est écouter les signes nager dans l'encre—tels vingt-six poissons aveugles—avant de naître au regard, c'est-à-dire de mourir en se fixant dans leur dernier cri d'amour; alors, dans l'essentiel, j'aurai dit ce que j'avais à dire et que chaque page savait déjà; c'est pourquoi la forme aphoristique est l'expression profonde du livre, car elle permet aux marges de respirer, car elle porte en soi la respiration du livre et exprime l'univers en une fois. Y 51.

p. 17: "What is given,": Eric Gould, "Godtalk," *Denver Quarterly* 15, no. 2 (summer 1980), p. 37.

p. 17: "be complete in itself,": Friedrich Schlegel, Athenaeums-Fragment 206: "Ein Fragment muss gleich einem kleinen Kunstwerke von der umgebenden Welt ganz abgesondert und in sich selbst vollendet sein wie ein Igel." Novalis: "Der Igel—ein Ideal . . . die grösste Masse Gedanken in den kleinsten Raum bringen." *Werke*, ed. Richard Samuel, vol. 3 (Darmstadt, Germ.: Wissenschaftliche Buchgesellschaft, 1965), p. 639.

p. 17: "Interruption is one,": Walter Benjamin, *Illuminations,* p. 151.

p. 18: "Only in fragments,": BM 42.
"C'est dans la fragmentation que se donne à lire l'immensurable totalité." LM 48.

p. 18: Michel Leiris: cf. interview in *Instants* 1 (1989), p. 43.

p. 18: "Mallarmé wanted to put,": Jabès, interview with Auster, *The Sin of the Book,* pp. 21–22.

p. 18: "meaning, perhaps, for the first time,": Robert Alter, *The Art of Biblical Narrative,* (New York: Basic Books, 1981), p. 12. Quoted in Susan Handelman, "Torments of an Ancient Word," in *The Sin of the Book,* p. 62.

p. 18: "lire aux éclats,": Ouaknin, *Concerto,* pp. 48–49 and passim.

p. 18: "for both Jabès and the rabbis,": Handelman, *The Sin of the Book,* p. 62.

p. 19: "The sky is blue,": Maurice Blanchot, *L'Entretien infini* (Paris: Gallimard, 1969), p. 14 (my translation).

p. 19: David Mendelson's false etymology: David Mendelson, "Table, livres, noms (judéo-égyptiens) jabèsiens," in *Jabès: Le livre lu,* ed. David Mendelson (Paris: Point hors Ligne, 1987), p. 23.

p. 19: "By turning their back,": ELLB 39.
Le peuple élu, en se détournant des Tables, donnait à Moïse une magistrale leçon de lecture. D'instinct—le Livre n'est-il pas antérieur à l'homme?—il hissait le viol de Dieu à hauteur de la première mort et, dressé contre la lettre, consacrait par son indépendance la brisure en laquelle Dieu S'écrit contre Dieu.
Le livre détruit donne à lire le livre. EL 47/8.

Edmond Jabès refers to this passage in the interview with Paul Auster, stressing the human need for the breaking: "[The Hebrew people] were not able to accept a word without origins, the word of God. It was necessary for Moses to break the book in order for the book to become human." *The Sin of the Book,* p. 23.

p. 19: "The Tablets of the Law,": Maurice Blanchot, "Le Livre des questions," *L'Amitié* (Paris: Gallimard, 1971), p. 254;
"The Book of Questions," trans. Paul Auster, in *The Sin of the Book,* p. 49.

p. 20: "Adam, or the Birth of Anxiety,": BS 25.
Et Dieu créa Adam.
Il le créa homme, le privant de mémoire.
Homme sans enfance, sans passé.

(Sans larmes, sans rires ni sourires.)
Homme surgi du Rien, ne pouvant même pas revendiquer une part de ce Rien. LP 37.

p. 20: "Reb Jacob,": BQ 85.
Reb Jacob croyait aussi à l'emphase qu'il comparait à la déchirure, avec ses faux anneaux d'eau, que fait la pierre tombée dans l'étang. La blessure se referme aussitôt. Ce sont les anneaux qui se reproduisent en s'agrandissant et qui témoignent—dérision—de l'ampleur du mal.

La parole divine est tue aussitôt prononcée. C'est à ses anneaux sonores, que sont nos paroles inspirées, que nous nous accrochons.

L'absence d'une parole divine la crée.

Au commencement de la parole, il y a l'emphase. Il y a l'écrasement céleste que nous subissons. L'écho meurt à mesure que la voix faiblit. La parole murmurée est humaine. LQ 92/3.

p. 20: "In every word,": The Zohar (III 20, 2a), quoted in A. Abécassis, "La lumière dans la pensée juive," in *Le thème de la lumière dans le Judaïsme, le Christianisme et l'Islam* (Paris: Berg International, 1976), p. 103.

p. 21: "Thus in Kabbalah,": Handelman, *The Sin of the Book*, p. 76.

p. 21: "To fragment,": ELLB 57.
Fragmenter le nom de Dieu qui est formé de tous les mots de la langue afin de le réduire à un mot, à une syllable, à une lettre. Ainsi avions-nous abordé, au bout de la nuit, l'alphabet.

Avec leurs morceaux épars, rétablir dans leur parenté nouvelle les Tables exemplaires. EL 68.

p. 21: "The fragment is not,": Jacques Derrida, "Edmond Jabès et la question du livre," in *L'écriture et la différence* (Paris: Editions du Seuil, 1967), p. 108 (my translation).

p. 22: "[Interruption] carries the mystery,": Maurice Blanchot, "Interruptions," trans. R. Waldrop, *The Sin of the Book*, pp. 44–45.

p. 22: "It is not only a word,": LBS 30.
" 'Ce n'est pas seulement un vocable que tu formes en l'écrivant, mais aussi un instant de ta vie que tu circonscris,' avait-il noté." PLS 36.

p. 23: Hegel, cf. Blanchot, *L'Entretien infini,* p. 49.

p. 23: "Logic can take care,": Ludwig Wittgenstein, *Tractatus Logico-Philosophicus,* trans. D. F. Pears and B. F. McGuinness (London: Routledge & Kegan Paul, 1961), p. 473.

p. 23: "symptomatic imitation,": Novalis and Wilhelm. von Humboldt, quoted in Antoine Berman, *L'Epreuve de l'étranger* (Paris: Gallimard, 1984), pp. 170, 244.

p. 23: "molten lava,": Haroldo de Campos, "Transluciferation," p. 12.

p. 23: "I cannot look,": A. W. Schlegel, "Nachschrift des Übersetzers," *Athenaeum: eine Zeitschrift*, ed. Curt Grützmacher, vol. 2 (Hamburg: Rowohlt, 1969), p. 107.

p. 24: "We can only write,": YEA 150.
Nous n'écrivons que ce qu'il nous a été accordé de lire et qui est une infime partie de l'univers à dire. Jamais le livre, dans son actualité, ne se livre. E 50.

p. 24: "Our lot is to interpret,": YEA 84.
"L'interpretation est notre lot dans un monde indéchiffrable." Y 116.

p. 24: "In the beginning,": Derrida, *L'écriture et la différence,* p. 102.

p. 24: "In the word *commentaire*,": ELLB 11.
"Dans *commentaire*, répétait-il, il y a les mots *taire, se taire, faire taire* qu'impose la citation." EL 15.

p. 24: "To comment on something,": DB 96.
En effet, commenter c'est faire taire un sens déjà établi, un sens figé. Mais c'est aussi faire taire la perception immédiate que nous avons du texte pour lui laisser une chance de parler par lui-même. DL 136.

p. 25: "It is not the commentary,": p. 69 (my translation).
"Ce n'est pas le commentaire qui commente, mais le texte qui l'a inspiré. Le commentaire est muet." P 69.

p. 25: "contain the object,": Berman, p. 244.

p. 25: "Every commentary,": DB 102.
"Tout commentaire est d'abord commentaire d'un silence." DL 142.

p. 25: "comment taire—comment être,": EL 13.

p. 25: "In the beginning is hermeneutics,": Derrida, *L'Ecriture et la différence,* p. 102 (my translation).
Cf. Nietzsche: "there are no facts, only interpretations." "Aus dem Nachlass," *Werke,* ed. Karl Schlechta, vol. 3 (Munich: Hanser, 1956), p. 903.

p. 25: "In the sense of the expression,": Ouaknin, *Concerto,* p. 79.

p. 26: "Even in 'normative' Judaism,": Handelman, *The Sin of the Book,* pp. 64–65.

p. 26: "The pages of the book,": BQ 25/6.
"Les feuillets du livre sont des portes. . . . L'âme est l'instant de lumière. . . . La distance est lumière . . ." LQ 25/27.

p. 26: *Voir, c'est*: LQ 19, 28, 42, LR 86; BQ 20, 27, 42, BR 63.

p. 27: "God: an endless word,": BR 48; LR 67.

p. 27: *"D'un mot à un mot,"*: LQ 43
"From one word to another,": BQ 42.

p. 27: "different from a,": Berman, *L'Epreuve de l'étranger*, p. 248

p. 27: "Translating . . . makes us,": Paul Valéry, "Variations sur les Bucoliques," *Oeuvres,* ed. Jean Hytier, vol. 1 (Paris: Gallimard, 1957), p. 215.

p. 28: The importance of this stage: see Justin O'Brien, "From French to English," in *On Translation,* ed. Reuben A. Brower (Cambridge, Mass.: Harvard University Press, 1959).

p. 28: the three stages of translation: Johann Wolfgang von Goethe, "West-Östlicher Divan: Noten und Abhandlungen," *Werke*, vol. 2 (Hamburg: Christian Wegner Verlag, 1949), pp. 255–56.

p. 28: as Lawrence Venuti has shown: see Venuti, *The Translator's Invisibility* (London: Routledge, 1996), pp. 5 ff. Venuti uses the terms "invisibility" and "transparency" negatively for translations that do not place the slightest obstacle between the reader and his native linguistic/cultural habits. Whereas Walter Benjamin, though in agreement with Venuti, uses "transparency" as praise: for not placing any obstacle between the reader and the foreign text; i.e., he applies it in the opposite direction. "A real translation is transparent; it does not cover the original, does not block *its* light." *Illuminations,* p. 79 (my italics).

p. 29: "towards a foreign likeness bent,": Schleiermacher; quoted in Venuti, *The Translator's Invisibility,* p. 101.

p. 29: "a higher and purer linguistic air,": Benjamin, *Illuminations,* p. 79.

p. 30: "it does not give us,": Novalis, "Blüthenstaub," #68, *Werke,* vol. 2, p. 439. Cf. also Berman, *L'Epreuve de l'étranger,* p. 172.

p. 30: "I am convinced,": Novalis, *Briefe und Dokumente*, ed. Ewald Wasmuth (Heidelberg: Lambert Schneider, 1954), pp. 366–68; quoted in Berman, *L'Epreuve de l'étranger,* p. 168.

p. 30: "ridiculous wooden sword,": LH 45 (my translation).
"Une ridicule épée de bois contre une virile épée de duel." LH 45.

p. 30: "A saber stroke,": ELLB 104.
Un coup de sabre dans le vide, c'est bien l'image que je souhaiterais laisser de ma vie et de mes écrits, disait-il. Et si quelques gouttes de mon sang ont, plus d'une fois, sali le sol, sache que chacune d'elles est un livre ignoré. EL 122.

p. 31: "is prodigious in that,": YEA 329.
Ma rue a ceci de prodigieux qu'elle est une rue dans toutes les rues du monde. Elle est pourtant petite et étroite. Dans le bâtiment qui abrite la poste et le télégraphe et qui s'élève en son milieu, elle subit une transformation qui lui ouvre les cinq continents. A 164.

p. 31: No wonder that he finds the word *rue*: ELLB 49, EL 59.

p. 33: "Involution,": Bounoure, *Edmond Jabès,* pp. 48, 53.

p. 34: the scream, the open wound: cf. BYRB 193.
"Le centre est le cri, la blessure vive, la clé." RL 57.

p. 34: "guérison par le livre,": Bounoure, *Edmond Jabès,* p. 62.

p. 34: "We are condemned,": Robert Oppenheimer, interview with Dr. Escoffier-Lambiotte, *Le Monde,* 29 April 1958; quoted by Marcel Cohen in *Ecrire le livre: autour d'Edmond Jabès*, Colloque de Cerisy-la-Salle, ed. Richard Stamelman and Mary Ann Caws (Seyssel, France: Champ Vallon, 1989), p. 260.

p. 35: that part of our literature: Marcel Cohen: "Cette extinction du récit, cette amputation irréparable subie par la littérature privée de son pouvoir de synthèse et qui sait, quand elle est consciente d'elle-même et de l'époque, qu'en maintenant l'apparence d'une cohérence, d'un sens, d'une destinée, elle n'anime que des fantômes. . . ." ibid., p. 259.

p. 35: "We write only,": YEA 150, E 50.

p. 35: "But . . . the spiral is,": Daniel Accursi, *La philosophie d'Ubu* (Paris: Presses Universitaires de France, 1999), p. 61 (my translation).

p. 35: "A young disciple,": Jabès, interview with Jason Weiss, in Jason Weiss, *Writing at Risk*, (Iowa City: Univ. of Iowa Press, 1991), p. 188. First printed in *Conjunctions* 9, (1986).

p. 35: "Everything is the same,": Gertrude Stein, *Selected Writings* (New York: Modern Library, 1962), p. 520.

p. 35: "*Cogitatio*,": Mary Carruthers, *The Book of Memory: A Study of Memory in Medieval Culture* (Cambridge: Cambridge Univ. Press, 1990), pp. 33–34

p. 37: *Néant, né en:* EL 35/36.

p. 37: "It is nothingness we are born in." ELLB 29/30.

p. 37: "Is it to this error,": YEA 178.
Dois-je inconsciemment à cette erreur de calcul, le sentiment que quarante-huit heures m'ont toujours séparé de ma vie? Les deux jours

ajoutés aux miens ne pouvaient être vécus que dans la mort. Ainsi, comme pour le livre, comme pour Dieu dans le monde, la première manifestation de mon existence fut celle d'une absence qui portait mon nom. E 93.

p. 37: "In any case, this error,": BR2 69.
Quoi qu'il en soit, à cette erreur de calcul que je n'ai jaimais voulu considérer comme telle mais, plutôt, comme un avertissement du hasard, je donnais, tant elle m'angoissait, une explication personnelle, y voyant la preuve concrète, fournie par l'inconscient, que *nous sommes plus vieux que notre vie. Le Livre des Questions* y puisa sa parole et, de ce vide avalisé, de ce hors-temps co-signé, a fait son lieu. . . . LR2 83.

p. 37: Jean Daive speaks of *arrière-absence*: Jean Daive, *Sous la Coupole* [*La Condition d'infini* 5], (Paris: P.O.L., 1996).

p. 38: "All this 'fore-speech,' ": Bounoure, *Edmond Jabès,* p. 74.

p. 38: "The threshold is perhaps death,": BR3 7.
"Le seuil c'est, peut-être, la mort." LR3 13.

p. 38: "as long as possible in a state of chaos,": DB 43.
"Cette matière, je tiens, le plus longtemps possible, à la préserver à l'état de chaos au seuil même du livre, afin que le lecteur puisse, lui aussi, assister à la naissance de l'ouvrage." DL 69.

p. 39: "ontic density,": Bounoure, *Edmond Jabès,* p. 74.

p. 39: "Yesterday, Elya,": YEA 182.
"Hier, Elya aurait fêté ses dix ans. E 98.

p. 39: "O Yaël, how I,": YEA 69.
"O Yaël, combien dans ma misère t'aurais-je aimée. . . . Tu aurais été à moi jusqu'à l'âme. . . ."
Je dirais: "Yaël . . ." comme si je m'adressais encore à elle. . . . "J'aurais voulu, Yaël, t'aider car, en le faisant, j'aurais été en harmonie avec mon âme. . . ." Y 95.

p. 40: "What if the word," BS 8, 27.
Et si, comme à l'homme, la parole mentait, aussi, à Dieu?

Notre notion de la vérité en serait, sérieusement, ébranlée," disait-il. LP 16.

p. 40: "What if Eve's sin,": BS 27.
Et si le péché d'Eve était, vraiment, celui de Dieu que celle-ci par amour pour Lui, prit à son compte? LP 40.

p. 40: the break with Egypt: cf. DB 25, DL 48.

p. 41: "This morning between rue Monge,": BYRB 134.
Ce matin, entre la rue Monge et la Mouffe, j'ai laissé le désert, après la rue des Patriarches et la rue de l'Epée-de-Bois, où s'élève ma demeure, envahir mon quartier. Le Nil n'était pas distant. LY 140.

p. 41: "There is a brooding,": Michael Palmer, "A Bonfire in the Starry Night," in *Irving Petlin: Le Monde d'Edmond Jabès* (Geneva: Galerie Jan Krugier, Ditesheim & Cie, 1998), p. 14.

p. 41: "At noon, he found himself,": BQ 55.
Il s'était retrouvé, à midi, face à l'infini, à la page blanche. Toute trace de pas, la piste avaient disparue. Ensevelies. LQ 56.

p. 41: "Whatever escapes us,": BQ 56.
"Ce qui nous dépasse nous détruit." LQ 57.

p. 42: "The Real,": BYRB 31.
"Le Réel qui est le sable et le Rien qui est l'azur sont mes deux horizons." LY 33.

p. 42: "The tree goes,": BQ 109.
"L'arbre tourne sur lui-même jusqu'à la cime et l'abeille autour de sa trompe. Reb Azar n'a-t-il pas écrit: 'Le chemin de la connaissance est plus rond qu'une pomme?' " LQ 117.

p. 42: "for we hold that 2 times 2,": BQ 92/3.
"Car nous témoignons que 2 fois 2 font aussi 5 ou 7 ou 9 . . . car nous sommes le tourment de la logique, dans l'addition des chiffres pairs, l'ordre et le désordre du nombre impair." LQ 99/100.

p. 43: as Didier Cahen records: Didier Cahen, *Edmond Jabès* (Paris: Pierre Belfond, 1991), p. 309.

p. 43: Leiris's biographer: Aliette Armel, *Michel Leiris* (Paris: Arthème Fayard, 1997), p. 169

p. 43: "all true closeness,": DB 12.
"Toute vraie proximité passe par la différence." DL 30.

p. 44: "I think poetry,":
Je crois que la poésie "jeu" a fait son temps et que l'on attend un poète à la fois averti et grave . . . Je suis heureux d'apprécier votre fougue, votre émotion, votre fougue-émotion; mais un cri n'est pas une oeuvre. J'ai peur que les mots en liberté soient un peu démodés. . . . [S]i vous essayiez de mettre tout cela en phrases-syntaxes!

Letter of 13 May 1935. Max Jacob, *Lettres à Edmond Jabès* (Alexandria: Editions du Scarabée, 1945), p. 15; quoted in Daniel Lançon, *Jabès l'Egyptien* (Paris: Jean Michel Place, 1998), p. 104 (my translation).

p. 44: "too tight,": DB 44.
"il les trouvait tantôt 'trop serrés', . . . tantôt 'trop lyriques'—'Lis les classiques pour leur pudeur,' m'écrivait-il—, tantôt 'trop laconiques'—'Lis du Chateaubriand pour la phrase.' " DL 70.

p. 44: "I am out of the world,": "Je suis hors du monde. Je ne puis subir que le martyre." Pierre Andreu, *Vie et mort de Max Jacob* (Paris: La Table Ronde, 1982), p. 256.

p. 44: the war years: cf. Cahen, *Edmond Jabès*, pp. 310–12; Lançon, *Jabès l'Egyptien*, pp. 148, 164.

p. 44: "A strange voyage,": Dominique Grandmont, *Le Voyage de Traduire* (Creil, France: Bernard Dumerchez, 1997), p. 9.

p. 45: "Writing is an act,": BS 31.
"Ecrire est un acte de silence, se donnant à lire dans son intégralité . . . Plus qu'au sens, attache-toi au silence qui a modelé le mot." LP 46, 45.

p. 45: "Silence is a form,": Claude Royet-Journoud, *A Descriptive Method*, trans. Keith Waldrop (Sausalito, Calif.: The Post-Apollo Press, 1995), p. 12.

p. 47: "a life-saving break,"; and "makes you feel,": DB 14.
"Le désert représentait donc pour moi une coupure salvatrice. Il répondait à un besoin urgent du corps et de l'esprit et je m'y enfonçais avec des désires tout à fait contradictoires: me perdre pour, un jour, me retrouver."
"Dans un pareil silence, la proximité de la mort se fait sentir d'une manière telle qu'il paraît difficile d'endurer davantage. Pour être nés dans le désert, seuls les nomades sont capables de supporter la pression d'un tel étau." DL 32/3.

p. 47: "[I]n traditional Judaism,": DB 65.
"dans le judaïsme traditionnel, j'ai privilégié ce qui passait par le livre et faisait des juif le peuple du livre. Là est ma vraie origine." DL 97.

p. 47: "There is no actor,": Nietzsche, *Genealogy of Morals*, vol. 1, section 13 (my translation).

p. 48: "is not so much the revelation,": Blanchot, *L'Entretien infini*, p. 187 (my translation). Cf. also DB 73, DL 108.

p. 48: "God will speak,": BYRB 86.
"C'est par la langue que nous parlons que Dieu nous parlera." LY 92.

p. 48: "the promised land,": Blanchot, *L'Entretien infini*, p. 187 (my translation).

p. 48: "We can no longer pronounce,": Jabès, interview with Philippe de Saint-Chéron, *La Nouvelle Revue Française* 464 (Sept. 1991), p. 68; quoted in Lançon, *Jabès, l'Egyptien*, p. 275.

p. 48: "The experience of the desert,": BM 172.
L'expérience du désert est, à la fois, celle du lieu de la Parole—où elle est souverainement parole—et celle du non-lieu où elle se perd à l'infini. LM 180.

p. 48: "A book is perhaps,": BR2 58.
Le livre est, peut-être, la perte de tout lieu; le non-lieu du lieu perdu. Un non-lieu, comme une non-origine, un non-présent, un non-savoir, un vide, un blanc. LR2 71.

p. 48: At the colloquium: Stamelman and Caws, eds., *Ecrire le livre,* p. 300. See also Lançon, *Jabès l'Egyptien,* p. 312, n. 34.

p. 49: "Il était dur, Picasso,": This information is also in Andreu, *Vie et mort de Max Jacob,* pp. 292–93. Andreu had published this information first in an essay on Jacob, in 1960. The friends were Pierre Colle and Henri Sauguet.

p. 49: "Je suis le livre." LR3 108. BR3 88,

p. 50: "What is a writer?" p. 54 (my translation).
"Qu'est-ce qu'un écrivain? Qu'est-ce qu'un juif? Juif et écrivain n'ont aucune image d'eux-mêmes à brandir. *'Ils sont le livre.'*" P 54.

p. 50: "I have been,": p. 38 (my translation).
"J'ai été ce mot." P 38.

p. 50: "A man of writing,": YEA 250.
L'homme d'écriture est l'homme des quatre lettres qui forment le Nom imprononçable. Dieu est absent par Son Nom. A 60.

p. 50: "Turning to the book,": YEA 168.
Aller au livre c'est, sans doute, avoir deviné qu'on allait, dans le vocable, se métamorphoser. . . ." E 78.

p. 50: "I took you in,": YEA 12.
Je te réçus, telle une parole. "Je" est le livre. Y 19.

p. 51: "Language, even though,": Bernard Noël; quoted in Grandmont, *Le voyage de traduire,* p. 87.

p. 52: "image of a place,": Jabès, to filmmaker Michelle Porte: "l'image d'un lieu, c'est l'image de l'Egypte," Lançon, *Jabès l'Egyptien,* p. 278.

p. 52: "The Jewish poet today,": Bounoure, *Edmond Jabès,* p. 104

p. 52: "A chessboard,": BQ 139.
Un damier est l'univers du citadin. As-tu remarqué que chaque case, noire ou blanche, répond à une case identique au ciel? Traverser un quartier, c'est aussi traverser une partie de la nuit ou du jour. Ici, tu es dans tel carrefour et à telle intersection imaginaire du vide. LQ 153.

p. 52: "The eyes sees nothing,": Jean Tortel: "l'oeil ne voit de l'objet que le nom," quoted in Francis Cohen, "Théâtre d'un non-lieu," *Je te continue ma lecture,* eds. M. Cohen-Halimi and F. Cohen (Paris: P.O.L., 1999), p. 212.

p. 53: "This absence of place,": BM 171.
Cette absence, en quelque sorte, de place, je la revendique. Elle confirme que le livre est mon seul lieu, à la fois le premier et l'ultime. Lieu d'un non-lieu, plus vaste, où je me tiens. LM 180.

p. 53: "This place is love,": BYRB 95.
"Ce lieu est amour. Il est absence de lieu." LY 101.

p. 53: "Ed, or the first mist,": Genesis 2:6 and Rachi's *Commentary*; quoted in BR 25, LR 37.

p. 53: "To write, now,": LH 9 (my translation).
Ecrire, maintenant, uniquement pour faire savoir qu'un jour j'ai cessé d'exister; que tout, au-dessus et autour de moi, est devenu bleu, immense étendue vide pour l'envol de l'aigle dont les ailes puissantes, en battant, répètent à l'infini les gestes de l'adieu au monde.
Oui, uniquement pour confirmer que j'ai cessé d'exister le jour où l'oiseau rapace a occupé seul l'espace de ma vie et du livre, pour régner en maître et dévorer ce qui, une fois encore, cherchait, en moi, à naître et que je tentais d'exprimer.
Inutile est le livre quand le mot est sans espérance. LH 9.

p. 54: "The whole surround,": C. D. Wright, in C. D. Wright and Carole Maso, "Conversation with Rosmarie Waldrop," *tripwire* 4 (winter 2000–01).

p. 54: "a mismatch, a disconnection,": Giorgio Agamben, *Idea of Prose*, trans. Michael Sullivan and Sam Whitsitt (Albany: State Univ. of New York Press, 1995), p. 40.

p. 55: "motivational space,": Hans-Georg Gadamer, "Man and Language," *Philosophical Hermeneutics*, trans. David E. Linge (Berkeley: Univ. of California Press, 1976), p. 67–68.

p. 55: "It is conceivable,": Ezra Pound, in *Pound's Cavalcanti,* ed. David Anderson (Princeton, N.J.: Princeton Univ. Press, 1983), pp. 12, 221.

p. 55: intentionality of a work: Walter Benjamin, *Illuminations*, pp. 74, 76.

p. 55: "World of expression,": Michèle Cohen-Halimi is actually speaking of the word, but it is even truer of the whole literary work: "Chaque mot implique un monde d'expression qui le précède, le soutient et lui permet en même temps qu'il l'en empêche de donner corps à ce qu'il veut dire. Le vers est tendu vers—la saisie compréhensive du corps singulier. Comment lire *ce* mot sans lire *le* mot? Le vers dépasse la visée du sens par la fiction d'une plénitude reconstituée. "Réduction projective," *Je te continue ma lecture,* p. 68 (my italics).

p. 55: "generalized Talmudism,": François Laruelle, "Edmond Jabès ou le devenir-juif," *Critique* 385/6 (June/July 1979); quoted by Helena Shillony in *Jabès: Le Livre lu en Israel*, ed. David Mendelson (Paris: Point hors Ligne, 1987), p. 107.

p. 56: *The Wedding Nights* (of Abd al-Rahmane al-Souyoûti), trans. René R. Khawam (Paris: Albin Michel, 1972). On the role of Arabic culture, see Jason Weiss, *Writing at Risk*, p. 180–85; Lançon, *Jabès l'Egyptien*, p. 277.

p. 56: "as if wanting to check,": DB 72.
"comme s'il s'agissait de certifier l'intuition que j'avais d'un certain judaïsme." DL 107.

p. 56: "It is clearly not the letter," DB 48.
. . . ce n'est évidemment pas la lettre de ces textes qui m'a marqué mais le moule de pensée, leur esprit profond, la logique si particulière. . . . DL 76.

p. 56: "they seem to try to go back,": Marcel Cohen: "[E.J.] ne laisse transparaître aucune filiation directe. . . . [E.J.], au contraire, semble bien parcourir un itinéraire inverse: tenter une remontée vers un en deçà de la littérature, vers cet instant où l'idée est encore prisonnière de sa gangue. . . ." "A propos de Sarah et de Yukel," in *Ecrire le livre: autour d'Edmond Jabès,* p. 53.

p. 57: Both Edmond and Arlette Jabès became French citizens in 1967. Somewhat different versions of the origin of their Italian nationality appear in Lançon, *Jabès l'Egyptien*, pp. 113–14, 172.

p. 58: "The poem holds its ground,": Paul Celan, "The Meridian," *Collected Prose,* trans. R. Waldrop (Manchester, England Carcanet, 1986), p. 49.
Es behauptet sich—erlauben Sie mir, nach so vielen extremen Formulierungen, nun auch diese—, das Gedicht behauptet sich am Rande seiner selbst; es ruft und holt sich, um bestehen zu können, unausgesetzt aus seinem Schon-nicht-mehr in sein Immer-noch zurück.
Dieses Immer-noch kann doch wohl nur ein Sprechen sein. Also nicht Sprache schlechthin und vermutlich auch nicht erst vom Wort her 'Entprechung.' . . .
Dieses Immer-noch des Gedichts kann ja wohl nur in dem Gedicht dessen zu finden sein, der nicht vergisst, das er unter dem Neigungswinkel seines Daseins, dem Neigungswinkel seiner Kreatürlichkeit spricht. *Der Meridian* (Frankfurt: S. Fischer, 1961), p. 17.

p. 58: *"übersetzt, übergesetzt,"*: Celan, letter to Renée Lang, 1954; quoted in Chris Chen, *tripwire* 2 (fall 1998), pp. 163 ff.

p. 58: "You are the one who writes,": BQ 11.
"Tu es celui qui écrit et qui est écrit." LQ 9.

p. 59: "Language is the,": Wilhelm von Humboldt, letter to Schiller; quoted in Berman, *L'Epreuve de l'étranger,* p. 229.

p. 59: "That which is always,": Giorgio Agamben, *Language and Death*, trans. K. E. Pinkus with M. Hardt (Minneapolis: Univ. of Minnesota Press, 1991), p. 25.

p. 59: "but the space around,": BQ 64.
"Mais, autour d'eux, il y a les signes de leurs origines qui grouillent." LQ 67.

p. 59: "The pages of the book,": BQ 25.
Les feuillets du livre sont des portes que les vocables franchissent, poussés par leur impatience à se regrouper, à retrouver leur transparence au bout de l'oeuvre traversée. . . . La lumière est dans leur absence que tu lis. LQ 25.

p. 60: "I am absent,": BQ 58.
"Je suis absent puisque je suis le conteur. Seul le conte est reel." LQ 60.

p. 60: "The writer is nobody." BQ 27, LQ 28.

p. 60: "The artist belongs,": Novalis, *Fragmente* II.2431, quoted in Berman, *L'Epreuve de l'étranger*, p. 126.

p. 60: "A bad book,": BM 11.
"Un mauvais livre n'est, peut-être, qu'un livre mal lu par son auteur." LM 17.

p. 60: "We can only write what we have been given to read,": YEA 150, E 50.

p. 60: All poetry is: Novalis, quoted in Berman, *L'Epreuve de l'étranger*, pp. 161, 158, 154.

p. 60: "The poet comes at language,": Valéry: "Le poète est une espèce singulière de traducteur qui traduit le discours ordinaire, modifié par une émotion, en 'langage des dieux.' " *Oeuvres*, vol. 1, ed. Jean Hytier (Paris: Gallimard, 1957), p. 212.

p. 60: "Writing a book,": YEA 36 (my italics).
Ecrire le livre, c'est associer sa voix à celle, virtuelle, des marges, c'est écouter les signes nager dans l'encre—tels vingt-six poisssons aveugles—avant de naître au regard. . . . ; alors, dans l'essentiel, j'aurai dit ce que j'avais à dire et que chaque page savait déjà. Y 51.

p. 61: "The meandering word,": BYRB 172.
"Le vocable, dans ses méandres, meurt de la plume; l'écrivain de la même arme retournée contre lui.
"De quel meurtre es-tu accusé? demandait Reb Achor à Zillieh, l'écrivain.

—Du meurtre de Dieu, répondit-il. Pour ma défense, cependant, j'ajouterai que je meurs avec Lui.' " RL 36.

p. 61: "It cannot name something,": Blanchot, *L'Entretien infini*, p. 60.

p. 62: "Indeed, I once thought,": ELLBn 34/5.
"—En effet, j'ai cru, une fois, trouver mon lieu dans mes paroles, puis . . .
. . . comment vous dire? Soudain, les mots se sont montrés dans leur différence.
—Je comprend mal.
—Voilà . . . comme si, tout à coup, je ne m'exprimais plus que par le silence dans cet espace laissé vacant par leur différence.
—Quelle différence?
— . . . quelque chose de fondamentalement incompatible entre l'homme et sa parole qui les tient à distance. . . .
—N'est-ce pas toujours les mots qui vous expriment?
—Sans doute, à l'instant où ma plume les dessine, où ma voix les libère . . . mais, aussitôt après, je m'aperçois que je n'ai pas écrit, que j'ai n'ai point parlé.
— . . . mais, alors, ce que vous lisez, ce que d'autres que vous entendent, qu'est-ce?
— . . . un entremêlement de sons, de vocables dans leur éloignement amer, dans leur vérité étrangère. L'homme est muet, vous dis-je. Il est la seule créature muette." EL 41/2.

p. 62: tattoos, arrows: BQ 59, LQ 61.

p. 62: "For I am writing,": BQ 33.
car je suis écriture
et toi blessure
T'ai-je trahi, Yukel?
Je t'ai sûrement trahí. LQ 34/5.

p. 62: "We grow old,": BYRB 196.
"Nous vieillissons par le verbe, nous mourons de nous traduire." RL 61.

p. 63: "Not resemblance,": Blanchot: "pas ressemblance, mais identité à partir d'une altérité." *Amitié,* p. 72.

p. 63: "Translating Pamuk,": Güneli Gün "Something Wrong with the Language," the Times Literary Supplement, (London), (12 March 1999), p. 14.

p. 63: "a double mirror,": BYRB 35.
"Un double miroir, dit-il, nous sépare du Seigneur; de sorte qu'en cherchant à nous voir, Dieu Se voit et que, cherchant à Le voir, nous ne voyons que notre visage." LY 37/8.

p. 64: "What is important,": (my translation).
Ce qui est important, vous savez, dans l'expérience du désert, c'est l'expérience de la voix, et, aussi, l'expérience de l'écoute. Dans le désert, vous entendez avant de voir, et les nomades peuvent même dire ce qui va surgir longtemps après. Je suis très sensible à ce phénomène d'écoute lié à la voix. A tel point que j'ai voulu distinguer la parole du livre des autres paroles. La parole du livre, *cette parole du silence,* je l'ai appelée vocable. *Ecrire le livre*, p. 308.

p. 64: took care of the synagogue: cf. Lançon, *Jabès l'Egyptien,* p. 50, p. 291, note 6.

p. 66: What neither Edmond nor Arlette talk much about: cf. Lançon, *Jabès l'Egyptien,* pp. 178–79, 194–95, 219–21, 250–59.

p. 66: "Strangely enough,": DB 51.
C'est un fait assez paradoxal, mais je me sentais plus proche—je pourrais dire plus dépendent—de la culture française au Caire qu'à Paris même. Il faut préciser que mon déracinement a été total et qu'il s'est pratiquement fait du jour au lendemain. . . . à Paris le sol se dérobait sous mes pieds. DL 79/80.

p. 67: ". . . the actual dialogue,": BD 7.
. . . le dialogue proprement dit, irremplaçable, vital mais qui, hélas, n'aura pas lieu, débutant au moment où nous prenons congé l'un de l'autre, rendus, tous deux, à notre solitude. LD 17.

p. 68: "When we converse,": José Ortega y Gasset, "The Misery and Splendor of Translation," trans. Elizabeth Gamble Miller, in *Theories of Translation,* ed. Rainer Schulte and John Biguenet (Chicago: Univ. of Chicago Press, 1992) p. 79. "Exchange of Words" BM 149; LM 157.

p. 68: "Insanity—the only insanity,": Celan; Daive, *Sous la coupole*, p. 104.

p. 69: "One letter,": ELLB 10.
"Il suffit d'une lettre commune pour que deux mots cessent de s'ignorer." EL 15.

p. 69: *écrit, récit:* ELLB 7, EL 11.

p. 69: *lettre, l'être:* DB 4.
"La lettre est à l'être ce que la mémoire est à l'oubli: à la fois le déroulement de son histoire et le sceau de son éternel sommeil." DL 19.

p. 69: "*feu-oeil* meant,": ELLB 69.
"*Feuille*, il écrivait: Feu-oeil; mais je n'ai jamis su si feu-oeil signifiait, pour lui, oeil défunt ou bien, au contraire, *oeil de feu*, ce qui correspond davantage à l'idée que je me fais de la page blanche sous l'oeil de laquelle se consume le vocable." EL 79.

p. 70: "the force of thinking,": Wilhelm von Humboldt, quoted in Berman, *L'Epreuve de l'étranger*, p. 243.

p. 70: "Reading Kabbalistic texts,": Ouaknin, *Concerto*, p. 330, n. 84.

p. 70: "The Surrealistic image" (and following): Jabès; "Ecrire c'est le contraire d'imaginer: Interview with Serge Fauchereau":
En fait, je suis visuel: je regarde les mots qui sont déjà une sorte d'image. Faisant corps avec le texte, l'image ne fonctionne plus pour moi comme une image. Ancrée dans la pensée, dans le développement, elle est un raccourci dans le discours, comme si elle n'était pas là pour elle-même mais par souci de précision. L'image surréaliste nous séduisait, nous frappait mais elle était autonome comme quelque chose "ajouté." *Instants* 1 (April 1989), p. 209.

p. 71: *lit aux éclats: Lire aux éclats*, Ouaknin, *Concerto*, p. 79.

p. 71: he finds the polysemic: Felix Philipp Ingold, *Und Jabès*, p. 126 f.

p. 71: " 'In the word *commentaire*,' ": ELLB 11.
"Dans *commentaire*, répétait-il, il y a les mots *taire, se taire, faire taire* qu'impose la citation." EL 15.

p. 71: *L'arbre est dans le marbre*: EL 79, ELLB 69.

p. 71: "Croire pour croître." LR 42.
"To have faith in order to fathom." BR 29.

p. 72: "Sans racines. Cent racines." EL 11.
"No roots. Grow roots." ELLB 7.

p. 72: ". . . écrit, récit,": ELLB 7.
. . . écrit, récit: un même mot dans le renversement naturel de l'ordre de ses lettres.
"Tout écrit nous propose sa part de récit," disait-elle. EL 11.

p. 72: homophonic Catullus translations: Celia and Louis Zukofsky, *Catullus* (London: Cape Goliard & Grossman, 1969).

p. 73: "his monstrous method,": Guy Davenport, "Zukofsky's English Catullus," in *Louis Zukofsky: Man and Poet*, ed. Carroll R. Terrell (Orono, Maine: The National Poetry Foundation, 1979), p. 367.

p. 73: " 'How can I know,' ": BQ 44.
Comment savoir si j'écris en vers ou en prose, notait Reb Elati, je suis le rhythme. LQ 45.

p. 73: "Lower limit speech,": Louis Zukofsky, "A 12," "A" (Berkeley: Univ. of California Press, 1978), p. 138.

p. 74: "Interruption always makes,": Bernard Noël, "L'interrupteur," in *Je te continue ma lecture*, p. 136.

p. 75: Lower limit scream: Cf. "In writing, truth is perhaps the scream." YEA 160.
"Dans's l'écrit, la vérité est, peut-être, le cri." E 66.

p. 77: "setting out to conquer,": BR 38.
"Partir à la conquête de l'inconnu n'est, peut-être, que la secrète espérance de découvrir sa ressemblance avec le connu." LR 54.

p. 78: "In the beginning,": BR 36.
"Au début était le verbe qui se voulait ressemblant." LR 50.

p. 78: " 'Can we be like Him,' ": BR 20.
"Peut-on ressembler à Celui qui, par essence, est sans ressemblance?" demandait reb Eliav.
Il lui fut répondu ceci: "Ne sommes-nous pas l'image du vide qui est sans image?" LR 31.

p. 78: "In front of the mirror,": BR 5, 23.
Devant le miroir, Sarah nue contemple son corps. Si elle s'attarde à l'examiner dans ses détails, c'est qu'elle sait qu'il lui échappe. . . . LR 12.
La pensée réinvente le corps. Le corps émergé est à l'image de la pensée; image—changeante—que nous entretenons.
Ton corps est un livre de pensées qui ne saurait se lire dans sa totalité. LR 34.

p. 79: Henri Peyre: in Cairo, cf. Lançon, *Jabès l'Egyptien*, p. 123.

p. 81: "Our text of origin,": BS 35.
. . . le texte d'origine: *le texte générateur de textes à écrire qui, bien que nous échappant toujours, ne cesse de nous hanter*? LP 51.

p. 81: "Man does not exist,": BYRB 236.
L'homme n'existe pas. Dieu n'existe pas. Seul existe le monde à travers Dieu et l'homme dans le livre ouvert. RL 100.

p. 81: "The non-question I am talking about,": Derrida, *L'Ecriture et la différence*, p. 114:
La non-question dont nous parlons, c'est la certitude inentamée que l'être est une Grammaire; et le monde de part en part un cryptogamme à constituer ou à reconstituer par inscription ou déchiffrement poétiques; que le livre est originaire, que toute chose est *au livre* avant d'être et pour venir *au monde*, ne peut naître qu'en *abordant* le livre, ne peut mourir qu'en échouant *en vue* du livre; et que toujours la rive impassible du livre est *d'abord*. (Derrida's italics)

p. 82: "Our lot is to interpret,": YEA 84.
"L'interprétation est notre lot dans un monde indéchiffrable." Y 116.

p. 82: "Your body is a book,": BR 23.
"Ton corps est un livre de pensées qui ne saurait se lire dans sa totalité." LR 34.

p. 82: "The aporia is here,": Giorgio Agamben, *Bartleby ou la création*, trans. Carole Walter (Saulxures, France: Circé, 1995), p. 29.

p. 83: "the meaning of the word,": Agamben, *Language and Death*, p. 25.

p. 83: "the only home,": (my translation).
"La seule demeure du peuple errant, la seule demeure du peuple juif, c'est la parole." Interview with Madeleine Chapsal, *L'Express* (18 April 1963), pp. 33–34, quoted in Lançon, *Jabès l'Egyptien*, p. 310, n. 18.

p. 83: "In the middle,": BYRB 97.
"Au milieu des vocables, il y a le vide par où ils s'évadent." LY 103.

p. 83: "In vain [the poet],": Bounoure, *Edmond Jabès*, pp. 36, 49.

p. 83: "the book where everything,": DB 15.
"Le livre, où tout est censé être possible à travers une parole que l'on croit pouvoir maîtriser, et qui s'avère n'être finalement que le *lieu* de sa faillite." DL 34.

p. 83: *"Negative Capability"*: John Keats, letter to George and Tom Keats, 21, 27? Dec. 1817.

p. 84: "Jabès's books are not obscure,": Richard Stamelman, "The Graven Silence of Writing," in *From the Book to the Book: An Edmond Jabès Reader* (Middletown, Conn.: Wesleyan Univ. Press, 1991).

p. 84: Maurice Blanchot: cf. DB 38, DL 63.

p. 84: "Your stories leave the grooves,": BM 78.
"Vos récits s'écartent des voies du récit pour ne plus être que la découverte de la parole à sa fin, à ses derniers instants audibles, inscrits." LM 86.

p. 84: "My wife and I,": Roger Laporte, "Un sourire mozartien," *Ralentir Trauvaux* 7 (winter 1997), my translation.

p. 84: "He read the manuscript,": DB 52.
C'est en 1962 qu'il lut le manuscrit du *Livre des Questions*. Il contribua à me rendre presque acceptable ce qui m'effrayait moi-même dans ces

pages. Il alla encore plus loin en me montrant que, mes contradictions étant la substance même de mes livres, il était vain de tenter de les éviter. DL 81.

p. 85: "Childhood is a piece of ground,": BQ 53.
L'enfance est une terre beignée d'eau sur laquelle flottent de petits bateaux en papier. Il arrive que les bateaux se transforment en scorpions; alors, la vie meurt par le poison à chaque instant.
Le poison est dans chaque corolle, comme la terre est dans le soleil. La nuit, la terre est livrée à elle-même, mais les hommes dorment heureusement. Dans le sommeil, ils sont invulnérables.
Le poison est le rêve. LQ 54.

p. 86: . . . a glass of wine: BQ 109, LQ 117.

p. 86: "There is no rest,": BR 56.
"Il n'y a point de repos au royaume des ressemblances." LR 78.

p. 87: for the Kabbalist: Gershom Scholem, *Major Trends in Jewish Mysticism* (New York: Schocken, 1961), p. 27.

p. 87: "shifters,": Roman Jakobson, *Selected Writings*, vol. 2, (The Hague: Mouton, 1971), p. 132.

p. 87: "The articulation—the shifting,": Agamben, *Language and Death,* p. 25.

p. 87: "invention bears on the production,": Adolfo Fernandez-Zoïla, *Le Livre, recherche autre d'Edmond Jabès* (Paris: Jean-Michel Place, 1978), p. 113.

p. 88: "I love to laugh,": Jabès: "j'aime rire, j'aime raconter des histoires, j'aime plaisanter. C'est une façon d'échapper à l'angoisse. . . ." *Ecrire le livre,* p. 305.

p. 89: difficult first years in Paris: cf. DB 35 f., DL 60.

p. 90: "Here the scream,": (UR 24 (my translation).
"Là, le cri est le personnage devenu cri; ailleurs, le rire est le monstre devenu rire." UR 24.

p. 90: "As for the cover,": Jabès, letter to R.W., 5 January 1973.

p. 93: " 'A double mirror,' " (and following passages): "Mirror and Scarf": BYRB 35–37, LY 37–40.

p. 96: "I was struck,"; and ". . . for the writer": (my translation).
Or j'ai été frappé par ce fait que si un peintre veut rendre la transparence, il ajoute des couleurs à une autre couleur. La couleur en soi, c'est l'opacité: pour la rendre cristalline, il faut ajouter une quantité de couleurs. Pour le peintre, la surcharge est transparence, alors que pour l'écrivain, au contraire, plus il efface, plus vite il arrive à l'essentiel. *Ecrire le livre,* p. 306.

p. 96: *des noms d'écoute*: Jabès; *Ecrire le livre*, p. 308.

p. 96: "You are a shape,": BQ 32/33.
"Tu es une forme qui se déplace dans le brouillard. . . . Tu es la parole éteinte au milieu des mensonges de l'anecdote." LQ 35.

p. 97: "Candidates for presence,": Bounoure, *Edmond Jabès*, p. 111.

p. 97: "White Space,": Bernard Noël, *Je te continue ma lecture,* p. 136.

p. 97: "I had planned,":"Je pensais travailler à ce texte pour Skira mais c'était compter sans 'Aely' dont je n'arrive pas à me détacher." Jabès, letter to R.W., 1 August 1971.

p. 97: The sand: " 'Pick up some sand,' wrote Reb Ivri, 'and let it glide between your fingers. Then you will know the vanity of words.' " BQ 113.
"Ramasse un peu de sable, écrivit Reb Ivri, puis laisse-le glisser entre tes doigts; tu connaîtras, alors, la vanité du verbe." LQ 122.
Cf. also Bounoure, *Edmond Jabès,* p. 49, 87.

p. 97: "The beginning of a garden,": "Out of a handful of sand we will make the beginning of a garden." BQ 133.
"D'une poignée de sable nous ferons un commencement de jardin." LQ 146.

p. 99: Edmond's trees: cf. BYRB 162, RL 25.

p. 99: "Anxiety of white and black,": BS 29.
Angoisse du blanc et du noir: Gris . . .
Lorsque, de noir qu'il était, tout a coup un mot écrit se retrouve gris, c'est que l'infini de la page l'a blanchi.
"O transparence!" disait-il.
Et il ajoutait, plus pour lui-même que pour les autres:
"La transparence, ah voilà le miracle. LP 42.

p. 99: "nothing is there,": Jabès, interview with Serge Fauchereau: "Rien ne se présente comme seulement bleu, par exemple; mais comme une possibilité de bleu. . . . Nous rassemblerons les images et les images des images jusqu'à la dernière qui est blanche et sur laquelle nous nous accorderons." *Instants* 1 (1989), pp. 212–13.

p. 99: "A symbol which interests us,": Susanne K. Langer, *Philosophy in a New Key* (New York: Mentor Books, 1948), p. 61.

p. 100: "To wait for words,": F 93.
"Attendre les mots qui réveilleront nos pensées en nous écrivant." ET 126.

p. 101: "And Reb Ardash,": BYRB 185.
"Ce n'est pas toujours le coeur qui clôt la boucle; ce sont quelquefois les dents. Il y a des morsures célestes qui témoignent du désespoir de Dieu." RL 49.

p. 101: "Quelle différence,": LQ 155, BQ 141.

p. 102: "Sais-tu,": A7, YEA 203.

p. 102: "the untranslatable is not this,": Berman, *L'Epreuve de l'étranger,* pp. 97–98.

p. 103: *les élans*: BQ 25, LQ 25.

p. 103: "tempo of its style,": Nietzsche, *Jenseits von Gut und Böse, Werke*, vol. 2.28, p. 593 f.

p. 103: "dissolve the Apollonian,": Haroldo de Campos, "Transluciferation," pp. 10–14.

p. 103: "set about the task,": Dilthey, quoted in Carl Dahlhaus, *Ludwig van Beethoven*, trans. Mary Whittall (Oxford: Clarendon Press, 1991), p. 4.

p. 104: "refers backward,": Gadamer, "Man and Language," p. 67.

p. 104: "We can write only,": BD 38.
"On ne peut écrire que sur ce silence." LD 61.

p. 104: "silence which has formed," (and following passages): BS 31.
"silence qui a modelé le mot. . . . Le silence du livre: une page que l'on lit. . . . Ecrire est un acte de silence, se donnant à lire dans son intégralité." LP 45/6.

p. 105: "four silver watchtowers,": BQ 74.

p. 106: "Leitwort style,": Ingold, ". . . schreiben heisst geschrieben werden . . . ," p. 136.

p. 107: "Palestinian workers from the hotel,": Ammiel Alcalay, "Desert Solitaire: Edmond Jabès, Resident Alien" [review of *A Foreigner Carrying in the Crook of his Arm a Tiny Book* and *The Book of Margins*], *Voice Literary Supplement* (Feb. 1994), p. 13. Reprinted in Ammiel Alcalay, *Memories of Our Future* (San Francisco: City Lights, 1999), pp. 55–60.

p. 108: "I have little taste for,": Jean Frémon, "Contre l'image?" in UR 10.

p. 109: "The *Midrash Konen*," (and following): Scholem, in *The Book, Spiritual Instrument*, eds. Jerome Rothenberg and David Guss (New York: Granary, 1996), pp. 137–39.

p. 109: "We always start out,": BM 40.
"Nous partons toujours du texte écrit pour revenir au texte à écrire, de la mer à la mer, du feuillet au feuillet." LM 46.

p. 109: "Fire, virginity of desire,": BM 38, 43.
Le feu est virginité du désir. . . . cette réponse proposée par un rabbin kabbaliste . . . et que détourné de son sens mystique originaire je soumets littéralement à votre réflexion; le Livre serait cela qui "est gravé avec le noir du feu sur le blanc du feu." Feu noir sur feu blanc. Consumation sans fin du parchemin sacré, du feuillet profane voués aux

signes, comme si ce qui est consigné—co-signé—écrit, n'était que jeu perpétré des flammes, feux de feux, "feux de mots", disiez-vous dans un récent entretien. Confiance en ce qui meurt purifié pour renaître du désir d'une mort purificatrice grâce à laquelle le vocable ajoute à sa lisibilité, la lisibilité d'un temps promu à la lecture "différée" dont on n'ignore plus qu'elle est lecture de toute lecture; temps toujours préservé dans le temps aboli. LM 44, 49/50.

p. 111: "If there is theory,": BR 18/19.
Si théorie il y a, elle est née d'un questionnement qui touche l'homme autant que le mot; l'homme à l'instant où il s'écrit; où il devient donc vocable. . . . Le prétendu auteur du Livre des Questions se souvient, aujourd'hui, de sa lente progression dans le livre et de son rejet par celui-ci: expulsion d'un lieu privilégié, où sa liberté s'exerçait aux dépens de son existence. LR 29.

p. 113: "The illegible lies in wait,": BR 1.
"L'illisibilité est au bout de la lisibilité perdante." LR 7.

p. 115: "Since then": Derrida: "Depuis, 'dans la production littéraire', comme vous dites, rien ne s'est formé qui n'ait son précédent quelque part dans le texte de Jabès." "Edmond Jabès aujourd'hui," in *Les nouveaux cahiers* 8, no. 31 (winter 1972/73), p. 56.

p. 118: "As if . . . the soul,": F 12.
. . . comme si—insistait-il—l'âme ne vibrait qu'à un seul son et que l'esprit ne s'enfiévrait qu'une fois. ET 25.

p. 118: "when we say 'I',": LH 35 (my translation).
". . . dire 'Je' c'est, déjà, dire la *différence*." LH 35.
"L'étranger,": ET 65.

p. 118: "emerge from and displace,": Handelman, *The Sin of the Book*, p. 77.

p. 118: "Reason, Cartesian 'common sense,' ": Accursi, *La philosophie d'Ubu*, p. 58.

p. 119: " 'A stranger twice over,' ": F 82.
Doublement étranger, disait-il, en tant qu'auteur d'un livre qu'il n'a pas

écrit et lecteur d'un livre qui l'écrit. Étranger au livre et à lui-même. ET 111.

p. 119: "to wait for words,": F93, ET 126.

p. 119: The diagrams: ELLB 52/53, EL 63.

p. 120: "The liber,": ELLB 54.
"Liber du tilleul, teille ou tille, dont on fait des cordes et des nattes, mais dont on s'est servi aussi pour écrire.
"Dans *liberté,* il y a le mot *liber* qui le récrit. Ainsi le mot *liberté* nous écrit dans la liberté du mot qui l'écrit," disait-il. EL 65.

p. 120: " 'Fin, *resurgit,*' ": EL 7.
"Our ears pick *fin*, 'the end,' out of the word *faim*, 'hunger.' The end is famished." ELLB 3.

" 'Dans les brumes,' ": EL 26.
" 'Out of the fog of the word *savoir*, 'to know,' looms the word *voir,* 'to see,' " he said. "Knowing is essentially seeing." ELLB 21.

"Néant: né on": EL 35.
"Néant : né en . . . It is nothingness we are born in. . . ." ELLB 29.

"Privé d'R": EL 39.
Deprived of the air of its r, *la mort*, death, dies asphyxiated in the word, *le mot*. ELLB 33.

"Dans le mot": EL 50.
"In the word *corps*, 'body,' " he said, "there rests the word *or,* 'gold'. . . ." ELLB 41.

"*Le mot* aérien": EL 89.
The airy, *aérien*, word is threatened form within by the word *rien,* by airy "nothing." ELLB 75.

"L'étranger?": ET 65.
The foreigner? The foreign I? F 43.

p. 121: "The unthinkable (impen*sable*),": p 98 (my translation).
L'impen*sable* n'est, peut-être, qu'un impensé auquel on a ajouté son lot de sable. P 98.

p. 122: "distance is the place,": Claude Royet-Journoud, *The Notion of Obstacle,* trans. Keith Waldrop (Windsor, Vt.: Awede, 1985), p. 57.

p. 123: "Mort rose,": EL 83, ELLB 71.

p. 123: As if his face: "The desert has no book." LBS 7.
"Le désert n'a point de livre". PLS 11.

p. 123: "Do you know,": LBS 43.
"Sais-tu—disait-il—ce qui, dans le désert, donne quelquefois aux grains de sable leur teinte grisâtre?—Ce n'est pas l'approche de la nuit mais, de nos livres sans lendemain, le voile de cendres qui les recouvre." PLS 49.

p. 123: "The ladder urges us,": BYRB 36.
"L'échelle nous presse de nous dépasser. Là est son importance. Mais, dans le néant, où la poser?" LY 39.

p. 123: "I rise,": BYRB 20.
"Je m'élève, mais là-haut il y a mon âme qui tente de prendre encore de la hauteur." LY 21.

p. 123: Merleau-Ponty points out: Maurice Merleau-Ponty, *Phénoménologie de la perception* (Paris: Gallimard, 1945), pp. 295–96.

p. 124: The paradox of self-reference: cf. Maurice Beebe, "Reflective and Reflexive Trends in Modern Fiction," *Bucknell Review* 22, no. 2 (1976), p. 14.

p. 124: Sees the paradox as equivocal: Rosalie Colie, *Paradoxia Epidemica* (Princeton, N.J.: Princeton Univ. Press, 1966), on "risk," p. 483.

p. 124: "Thinking means contradicting,": Accursi, *La philosophie d'Ubu*, p. 58.

p. 125: "Are we not,": BR 20.
"Ne sommes-nous pas l'image du vide qui est sans image?" LR 31.

p. 125: "My name is in my pain,": BYRB 118.
"Mon nom est dans ma peine et ma peine n'a pas de nom." BY 124.

p. 125: "The more I care,": BYRB 56.
Plus je tiens à ce que j'écris, plus je me coupe des sources de mes écrits. Plus je me veux sincère, plus vite il me faut abandonner l'initiative aux mots, car je ne puis leur refuser d'exister sans moi. Je suis pourtant à l'origine de leur existence. Je suis donc celui qui a conçu l'être verbal qui aura son propre destin dont dépend mon destin d'écrivain. LY 60.

p. 126: "In creating, you create,": BR2 104.
En créant, tu crées l'origine où tu t'abîmes. LR2 124.My translation loses the suggestion of infinite regress, of *mise en abîme*.

p. 126: "You comment on your commentary,": BYRB 158.
Tu commentes ton commentaire et, ainsi de suite, jusqu'à n'être plus que l'arrière-petit-fils de ton fils. RL 21.

p. 126: "God is sculpted." BYRB 36.
"Dieu est sculpté." LY 39.

p. 126: "the origin is,": Jabès, Colloque de Cerisy: "l'acte d'écrire est un acte du futur: on est toujours en avant. Pourquoi? Parce que l'origine n'est pas derrière nous mais elle est devant." *Ecrire le livre*, p. 304.

p. 127: Is this mysticism: Giancarlo Carabelli, "L'esperienza della scrittura," *Tempo Presente* (June 1964), pp. 41–48.

p. 127: "When God, *El*,": ELLB 3.
"Dieu, *El*, pour se révéler, Se manifesta par un point." EL 7.

p. 127: "God refused image,": ELLB 15.
"Dieu refusa l'image, refusa la langue, afin d'être Soi-même le point." EL 19.

p. 127: "God only repeats God,": BR 1.
Dieu ne répète que Dieu: mais l'homme? Ah l'homme répète aussi Dieu. LR 7.

p. 128: "But for those,": YEA 10.
Mais pour ceux, épris d'absolu que l'éternité obsède, aller à Dieu pour l'adorer ou le détruire, c'est atteindre le fond de la détresse humaine; car notre désespoir est dans l'acte qui nous conduit à revendiquer la mort de Dieu afin de L'aimer plus que nous, contre nous-mêmes. Y 16.

p. 128: "Deprived of God,": YEA 143.
Privé de Dieu, dans l'équivoque de Sa mort, où le destin de la créature est dessein baroque d'écriture. E 40.

p. 129: "To write as if,": YEA 153.
Ecrire, comme si l'on s'adressait à Dieu; mais qu'attendre du néant où toute parole est désarmée? E 55.

p. 129: "God's being beyond conditions,": BM 191.
L'incondition de Dieu est donc tributaire de cette première et ultime évidence; la condition même de son incondition: *n'être pas*. LM 200.

p. 129: " 'Can we be,' ": BR 20.
Peut-on ressembler à Celui qui, par essence, est sans ressemblance? demandait reb Eliav. Il lui fut répondu ceci: 'Ne sommes-nous pas l'image du vide qui est sans image?' LR 31.

p. 129: "A double mirror,": BYRB 35.
Un double miroir, dit-il, nous sépare du Seigneur; de sorte qu'en cherchant à nous voir, Dieu Se voit et que, cherchant à Le voir, nous ne voyons que notre visage. LY 38.

p. 130: "Was it me,": YEA 68/9.
Etait-ce moi ou *l'autre* qui l'enlaçait? *L'autre,* sans doute, à qui Yaël s'adressait chaque fois avec tant de complaisance dans la voix et dans les yeux, que j'en souffrais profondément. Cependant, ce matin ou ce soir là, je ne sais plus, il se produisit une chose étonnante à laquelle je ne cesse de penser. Je n'étais plus le même. Je n'étais plus moi. J'étais *l'autre* ou plutôt je prenais enfin la place qu'il occupait et j'en éprouvais une telle exaltation, j'étais si plein de reconnaissance pour l'heure qui

me favorisait et pour le monde, que je perdis le contrôle de mes actes et serrai Yaël contre moi si longtemps qu'elle s'écroula, inanimée. Y 94.

p. 130: "First, my relations,": YEA 89.
Mes relations avec *l'autre*. Elles ont commencé dans le regard de Yaël détourné, soudain, de son objet pour embrasser le monde où je n'étais plus. Y 124.

p. 130: "between me and me," YEA 98.
"Entre moi et moi, Yaël ne sait choisir." Y 137.

p. 131: "You are hostile,": YEA 97.
Ton hostilité à mon égard, est celle que tu ressens pour tout ce que tu n'as pas créé.
Tu n'acceptes que ce qui t'est venu de toi. Tu ne prends que ce qui t'est remis de tes mains.
Tu aimes *l'autre,* non pour lui-même, mais contre moi. Y 136.

p. 131: "I was no longer,": YEA 70.
Je n'étais plus *l'autre*. Il était debout, derrière moi. Je compris que l'immense distance que Yaël avait voulu mettre entre nous, abolissant celle qui apparemment existait entre *l'autre* et moi, de sorte que j'étais le cauchemar contre lequel elle luttait en se cramponnant à son amant, par-delà mes mains qui ne lâchaient plus son cou. Y 96.

p. 132: "to be onself in the other,": YEA 105.
"être soi-même en *l'autre* . . ." Y 146.

p. 132: ". . . you said to me,": YEA 91.
. . . tu me dis: "est-ce toi?" Pris au jeu, je te répondis: "Non." Tu te jetas, alors, dans les bras de *l'autre* en hurlant: "Il change. Il est bien forcé de changer aussi. Ce n'est pas lui. C'est toi." Y 127.

p. 132: "You will die,": YEA 109.
Tu mourras dans le livre où je meurs avec *l'autre,* après Dieu. Y 152.

p. 132: "In the first mirror,": YEA 49.
Dans le premier miroir, ô femme, s'est delecté le mensonge.
Dans le second miroir, ô femme, a éclaté le mensonge.
Dans le troisième miroir, ô femme, la vérité s'interroge. Y 67.

p. 133: the earthly paradise: "The earthly paradise was asleep in the mirrors." YEA 21.
"Le paradis terrestre dormait dans les miroirs." Y 31.

p. 133: "the alternating of All,": YEA 41.
"l'alternance du Tout et du Rien que masque l'apparance." Y 58.

p. 133: "the lie of images,": YEA 41.
"le mensonge de l'image. Miroir d'un miroir, l'univers vit de ses reflets." Y 58.

p. 133: "Beings and things,": YEA 114/5.
L'être, la chose n'existent que dans le miroir qui les contrefait. Nous sommes les innombrables facettes de cristal où le monde se reflète et nous renvoie à nos reflets; de sorte que nous ne pouvons nous connaître qu'à travers l'univers et le peu qu'il a retenu de nous. Y 161.

p. 134: "It is a assumed here,": D. W. Winnicott, *Playing and Reality,* p. 13.

p. 134: "The Spirit is,": Dickinson, *The Poems of Emily Dickinson,* ed. Thomas H. Johnson (Cambridge, Mass.: Harvard Univ. Press, 1958), p. 733.

p. 134: "He regularly makes his rounds,": Daive, *Sous la Coupole,* pp. 116–17 (my translation).

p. 136: John Taggart has dramatized this: John Taggart, "Walk-Out: Rereading George Oppen," *Chicago Review* 44, no. 2 (1998), pp. 29–94.

p. 137: "Nous n'écrivons,": E50, YEA 150.

p. 138: "All translators live,": Blanchot, "Traduire," in *L'Amitié*, p. 71 (my translation).

p. 138: Marcel Cohen . . . recalls Edmond: Marcel Cohen, "Quatre Anamnèses," in *EJ* (Paris: Jean-Luc Poivret Edition, 1991), p. 30.

p. 140: Edmond Jabàs, *Désir d'un commencement Angoisse d'une seule fin* (Montpellier, France: Fata Morgána, 1991), pp. 13, 15.

p. 141: "From the point of view,": Jakobson and Bogatyrev; quoted in Giorgio Agamben, *Image et Memoire*, trans. Gilles A. Tiberghien (Paris: Ed. Hoebeke, 1998), p. 52.

p. 142: "What then, is this,": DB 103.
Qu'est-ce, alors, que cette parole initiale? Peut-être une absence insupportable de parole que celle-ci viendra, à notre insu, combler en s'exposant. DL 144.

p. 143: "I don't presume,": Jabès, interview with Paul Auster, in *The Sin of the Book*, p. 20.

p. 144: "My landscape is the desert,": UR 59 (my translation).
Mon paysage est le désert. J'ai grandi avec ce paysage devant les yeux—mais est-ce un paysage?—avant de me perdre en lui. Il n'y a pas de couleurs dans le désert. Il y a l'infini de la couleur. La couleur, dans le désert, ne retient pas le regard, ne l'arrête pas. Elle se laisse traverser par lui. Transparence. Nudité. De là est né, peut-être, mon peu de goût pour les images; mais c'est plus compliqué que cela. UR 59.

p. 144: "Against the Image?": Jean Frémon, UH 13/15.

p. 145: "It is often said,": Antonio R. Damasio: *Descartes' Error: Emotion, Reason, and the Human Brain* (New York: Avon Books, 1994), p. 106.

p. 146: "Your eyes lived,": Barbara Einzig, "Aduwa," *Conjunctions* 17 (1991), pp. 178, 180.

p. 150: "Mark the first page,": BQ 13.
Marque d'un signet rouge la première page du livre, car la blessure est invisible à son commencement. LQ 11.

p. 150: "My first images,": (my translation).
Mes premières images ont été des images d'Orient, et mon paysage, un paysage d'Orient. Mais je ne suis pas resté de ce coté-là du visible. Trop séduisante, trop captivante, la poésie orientale est pareille à une fresque. Et je m'intéresse aussi à l'envers de la fresque, à l'envers du mur. Lançon, *Jabès l'Egyptien*, p. 312, n. 34.

p. 150: "It is in some way,": Lançon, ibid., p. 277.

p. 150: On the first day: cf. A. Abécassis, "La lumière dans la pensée juive," pp. 7–10, 32.

p. 151: "We always search,": Dominique Grandmont, *Le Voyage de Traduire*, pp. 76–77.

p. 153: "prefer'd exquisite flowering,"; "giddy little manic": Michael Gizzi, *Species of Intoxication*, (Providence, R.I.: Burning Deck, 1983), pp. 62, 63.

p. 154: "There is no place,": BR2 58.
Il n'y a pas de lieu qui ne soit reflet d'un autre lieu; c'est ce lieu reflété qu'il importe de découvrir. Il est lieu dans le lieu. J'écris dans la dépendance de ce lieu. LR2 71.

p. 154: "There was a place,": UR 81 (my translation).
"Il y avait un lieu. C'est dans ce 'il y avait' qu'elle se situe; dans cette absence à explorer." UR 81.

p. 155: *Ma langue maternelle* /"My mother tongue,": cf. LD 87, BD 55.

p. 155: like memory for Aristotle: Carruthers, *The Book of Memory,* p. 56.

BIBLIOGRAPHY

Abécassis, Armand "La lumière dans la pensée juive," in *Le thème de la lumière dans le Judaïsme, le Christianisme et l'Islam,* Paris: Berg International, 1976.

Abraham, Nicolas. *Rhythms*, trans. Benjamin Thigpen and Nicholas T. Rand, Stanford, Calif.: Stanford Univ. Press, 1995.

Accursi, Daniel. *La philosophie d'Ubu*, Presses Universitaires de France, 1999.

Agamben, Giorgio. *Language and Death,* trans. K. E. Pinkus with M. Hardt, Minneapolis: Univ. of Minnesota Press, 1991.

———, *Idea of Prose*, trans. Michael Sullivan and Sam Whitsitt, Albany: State Univ. of New York Press, 1995.

———, *Bartley ou la création*, trans. Carole Walter, Saulxures, France: Circé, 1995.

———, *Homo Sacer I: Le pouvoir souverain et la vie nue,* trans. Marilène Raiola, Paris: Editions du Seuil, 1997.

———, *Image et Memoire*, trans. Gilles A. Tiberghien, Paris: Ed. Hoebeke, 1998.

Alcalay, Ammiel. "Desert Solitaire: Edmond Jabès, Resident Alien" [review of *A Foreigner Carrying in the Crook of His Arm a Tiny Book* and *The Book of Margins*], *Voice Literary Supplement* (Feb. 1994). Reprinted in *Memories of Our Future*, San Francisco: City Lights, 1999, pp. 55–60.

Anderson, David. ed. *Pound's Cavalcanti,* Princeton, N.J.: Princeton Univ. Press, 1983.

Andreu, Pierre. *Vie et mort de Max Jacob,* Paris: La Table Ronde, 1982.

Armel, Aliette. *Michel Leiris*, Paris: Arthème Fayard, 1997.

Auster, Paul. "Interview with Edmond Jabès," *Montemora* 6 (1979). Reprinted in *The Sin of the Book*, ed. Eric Gould, Lincoln: Univ. of Nebraska Press, 1985.

Beebe, Maurice. "Reflective and Reflexive Trends in Modern Fiction," *Bucknell Review* 22, no. 2 (1976).

Benjamin, Walter. "The Task of the Translator," in *Illuminations,* ed. Hannah Arendt, trans. Harry Zohn, New York: Schocken, 1969.

Berman, Antoine. *L'Epreuve de l'étranger*, Paris: Gallimard, 1984.

Blanchot, Maurice. *L'Entretien infini,* Paris: Gallimard, 1969.

———, *L'Amitié,* Paris: Gallimard, 1971.

Bounoure, Gabriel. *Edmond Jabès: la demeure et le livre,* Montpellier, France: Fata Morgana, 1984.

Cahen, Didier. *Edmond Jabès*, Paris: Pierre Belfond, 1991.

Carabelli, Giancarlo. "L'esperienza della scrittura," *Tempo Presente* (June 1964).

Carruthers, Mary. *The Book of Memory: A Study of Memory in Medieval Culture*, Cambridge: Cambridge Univ. Press, 1990.

Celan, Paul. *Collected Prose*, trans. R. Waldrop, Manchester, England: Carcanet, 1986.

Chen, Chris. "The Afterlife of the Poem: an Appreciation of Paul Celan," *tripwire* 2 (fall 1998).

Cohen, Josh. "Infinite Desertion: Edmond Jabès, Maurice Blanchot and the Writing of Auschwitz" (*forthcoming article*).

Cohen, Marcel, and Dominique Fourcade, Didier Cahen, Joseph Guglielmi. *E J,* Paris: Jean-Luc Poivret Edition, 1991.

Cohen-Halimi, Michèle and Francis Cohen, eds. *Je te continue ma lecture,* Paris: P.O.L., 1999.

Colie, Rosalie. *Paradoxia Epidemica,* Princeton, N.J.: Princeton Univ. Press, 1966.

Dahlhaus, Carl. *Ludwig van Beethoven*, trans. Mary Whittall, Oxford: Clarendon Press, 1991.

Daive, Jean. *Sous la Coupole* (La Condition d'infini, 5), Paris: P.O.L., 1996.

Damasio, Antonio R. *Descartes' Error: Emotion, Reason, and the Human Brain,* New York: Avon Books, 1994.

de Campos, Haroldo. "Transluficeration," *Ex* 4 (1985).

Derrida, Jacques. *De la grammatologie*, Paris: Editions de Minuit, 1967.

———, *L'écriture et la différence,* Paris: Editions du Seuil, 1967.

———, "EJ aujourd'hui," in *Les nouveaux cahiers* 8, no. 31 (winter 1972–73).

Einzig, Barbara. "Aduwa," *Conjunctions* 17 (1991).

Fernandez-Zoïla, Adolfo. *Le Livre, recherche autre d'Edmond Jabès,* Paris: Jean-Michel Place, 1978.

Frémon, Jean. "Contre l'image?" in *Un regard,* Montpellier, France: Fata Morgana, 1992.

Gadamer, Hans-Georg. "Man and Language," *Philosophical Hermeneutics,* trans. David E. Linge, Berkeley, Univ. of California Press, 1976.

Gizzi, Michael. *Species of Intoxication*, Providence, R. I.: Burning Deck, 1983.

Goethe, Johann Wolfgang von. "West-Östlicher Divan: Noten und Abhandlungen," *Werke*: "Hamburger Ausgabe," vol. 2, Hamburg: Christian Wegner Verlag, 1949.

Gould, Eric, ed. *The Sin of the Book*, Lincoln: Univ. of Nebraska Press, 1985.

———, "Godtalk," *Denver Quarterly* 15, no. 2 (summer 1980), p. 37.

Grandmont, Dominique. *Le Voyage de Traduire,* Creil, France: Bernard Dumerchez, 1997.

Groborne, [Robert]. *Une lecture . . .*, Évreux, France: Æncrages & Co., 1981.

Guglielmi, Joseph. *La Ressemblance impossible: Edmond Jabès,* Paris: Les Editeurs Français Réunis, 1978.

Handelman, Susan. 'Torments of an Ancient Word," in *The Sin of the Book,* ed. Eric Gould, Lincoln: Univ. of Nebraska Press, 1985.

Hocquard, Emmanuel. "Blank Spots," trans. Stacy Doris, *Boundary2* 26, no. 1 (spring 1999).

Ingold, Felix Philipp. ". . . schreiben heisst geschrieben werden . . . ," in *Und Jabès*, ed. Jutta Legueil, Stuttgart: Verlag Jutta Legueil, 1994.

Jacob, Max. *Lettres à Edmond Jabès*, Alexandria, Egypt: Editions du Scarabée, 1945.

Jakobson, Roman. *Selected Writings*, vol. 2, The Hague: Mouton, 1971.

Lançon, Daniel. *Jabès l'Egyptien*, Paris: Jean Michel Place, 1998.

Langer, Susanne K. *Philosophy in a New Key*, New York: Mentor Books, 1948.

Laporte, Roger. "Un sourire mozartien," *Ralentir Trauvaux* 7 (winter 1997).

Leiris, Michel. Interview, *Instants* 1 (1989).

Mendelson, David, ed. *Jabès: Le livre lu en Israel,* Paris: Point hors Ligne, 1987.

Merleau-Ponty, Maurice. *Phénoménologie de la perception*, Paris: Gallimard, 1945.

Mosès, Stéphane. "Son nom de cristal," *Instants* 1(1989).

Nietzsche, Friedrich Wilhelm. *Werke,* ed. Karl Schlechta, Munich: Hanser, 1956.

Novalis, *Werke*, ed. Richard Samuel, Darmstadt, Germ.: Wissenschaftliche Buchgesellschaft, 1965.

———, *Briefe und Dokumente*, ed. Ewald Wasmuth, Heidelberg: Lambert Schneider, 1954.

O'Brien, Justin. "From French to English," in *On Translation*, ed. Reuben A. Brower, Cambridge: Harvard Univ. Press, 1959.

Ortega y Gasset, José. "The Misery and Splendor of Translation," trans. Elizabeth Gamble Miller, in *Theories of Translation,* ed. Rainer Schulte and John Biguenet, Chicago: Univ. of Chicago Press, 1992.

Ouaknin, Marc-Alain. *Concerto pour quatre consonnes sans voyelles,* Paris: Payot & Rivages, 1998.

Palmer, Michael. "Un feu de joie dans la nuit étoilée," in *Irving Petlin: Le Monde d'Edmond Jabès,* Geneva: Galerie Jan Krugier, Ditesheim & Cie, 1998.

Royet-Journoud, Claude. *A Descriptive Method*, trans. Keith Waldrop, Sausalito, Calif.: The Post-Apollo Press, 1995.

———, *The Notion of Obstacle,* trans. Keith Waldrop, Windsor, Vt: Awede, 1985.

de Saint-Chéron, Philippe. Interview, *La Nouvelle Revue Française* 464 (Sept. 1991).

Schlegel, A. W. "Nachschrift des Übersetzers," in *Athenaeum: eine Zeitschrift*, vol. 2, ed. Curt Grützmacher, Hamburg: Rowohlt, 1969.

Scholem, Gershom. *Major Trends in Jewish Mysticism,* New York: Schocken, 1961.

———, "The Oral and the Written," in *The Book, Spiritual Instrument,* eds. Jerome Rothenberg and David Guss, New York: Granary, 1996.

Stamelman, Richard, and Mary Ann Caws, eds. *Ecrire le livre: autour d'Edmond Jabès*, Colloque de Cerisy-la-Salle, Seyssel, France: Champ Vallon, 1989.

Stamelman, Richard. "The Graven Silence of Writing," in *From the Book to the Book: An Edmond Jabès Reader*, Middletown, Conn.: Wesleyan Univ. Press, 1991.

Stein, Gertrude. *Selected Writings,* New York: Modern Library, 1962.

Taggart, John. "Walk-Out: Rereading George Oppen," *Chicago Review* 44, no. 2 (1998).

Terrell, Carroll R., ed. *Louis Zukofsky: Man and Poet*, Orono, Maine: The National Poetry Foundation, 1979.

Valéry, Paul. "Variations sur les Bucoliques," *Oeuvres,* ed. Jean Hytier, Paris: Gallimard ("Bibliothèque de la Pléiade"), 1957.

Venuti, Lawrence. *The Translator's Invisibility*, London: Routledge, 1996.

Weiss, Jason. *Writing at Risk*, Iowa City: Univ. of Iowa Press, 1991.

Winnicott, D. W. *Playing and Reality,* New York: Tavistock, 1989.

Wittgenstein, Ludwig. *Tractatus Logico-Philosophicus,* trans. D. F. Pears and B. F. McGuinness, London: Routledge & Kegan Paul, 1961.

Zukofsky, Louis. "A 12," "A," Berkeley: Univ. of California Press, 1978.

About the author:

Rosmarie Waldrop has translated forteen volumes of Edmond Jabès's work, most recently *Desire for a Beginning / Dread of One Single End* (Granary Books, 2001). Recent books of poetry are *Reluctant Gravities* (New Directions, 1999), *Split Infinites* (Singing Horse Press, 1998), and *Another Language: Selected Poems* (Talisman House, 1997). Northwestern Univ. Press has reprinted her two novels, *The Hanky of Pippin's Daughter* and *A Form/of Taking/It All* in one paperback. She lives in Providence, Rhode Island where she co-edits Burning Deck books with Keith Waldrop.